AAT

Qualifications and Credit Framework (QCF)

AQ2013

LEVEL 3 DIPLOMA IN ACCOUNTING

COMBINED TEXT AND QUESTION BANK

Indirect Tax
FA 2015 (1)

2015 Edition

For assessments from January 2016

Third edition August 2015
ISBN 9781 4727 2179 2

Previous edition
ISBN 9781 4727 0913 4

British Library Cataloguing-in-Publication Data
A catalogue record for this book is available from the British
Library

Published by
BPP Learning Media Ltd
BPP House
Aldine Place
London
W12 8AA

www.bpp.com/learningmedia

Printed in the United Kingdom by Martins of Berwick
Sea View Works
Spittal
Berwick-Upon-Tweed
TD15 1RS

We are grateful to the AAT for permission to reproduce the AAT
sample assessment(s) and the reference material for the AAT
assessment of Indirect Tax. The answers to the AAT sample
assessment(s) have been published by the AAT. All other answers
have been prepared by BPP Learning Media Ltd.

CONTENTS

BPP note: Assessments under FA 2014 will cease to be available from 31 December 2015. Assessments under FA 2015 will be available from January 2016. This Text edition includes the provisions of FA 2015. Please ensure you check the date you intend to sit your assessment to ensure you are using the correct material.

BPP LEARNING MEDIA'S AAT MATERIALS

The AAT's assessments fall within the **Qualifications and Credit Framework** and most papers are assessed by way of an on demand **computer-based assessment**. BPP Learning Media has invested heavily to ensure our materials are as relevant as possible for this method of assessment. In particular, our **suite of online resources** ensures that you are prepared for online testing by allowing you to practise numerous online tasks that are similar to the tasks you will encounter in the AAT's assessments.

Resources

The BPP range of resources for Indirect Tax comprises:

- **Combined Text and Question Bank**, the first part of which covers all the knowledge and understanding needed by students, with numerous illustrations of 'how it works', practical examples and tasks for you to use to consolidate your learning. The majority of tasks within the texts have been written in an interactive style that reflects the style of the online tasks we anticipate the AAT will set. At the back of this **Combined Text and Question Bank** there are additional learning questions plus the AAT's sample assessment(s) and a number of BPP full practice assessments. Full answers to all questions and assessments, prepared by BPP Learning Media Ltd, are included.

  When you purchase a Combined Text and Question Bank you are also granted free access to its content online.

- **Passcards**, which are handy pocket-sized revision tools designed to fit in a handbag or briefcase to enable you to revise anywhere at anytime. All major points are covered in the Passcards which have been designed to assist you in consolidating knowledge.

- **Lecturers' resources**, for units assessed by computer based assessments. These provide a further bank of tasks, answers and full practice assessments for classroom use, available separately only to lecturers whose colleges adopt BPP Learning Media material.

This Combined Text for Indirect Tax has been written specifically to ensure comprehensive yet concise coverage for the AAT's **AQ2013** learning outcomes and assessment criteria.

Each chapter contains:

- Clear, step by step explanation of the topic

- Logical progression and linking from one chapter to the next

- Numerous illustrations of 'how it works'

- Interactive tasks within the text of the chapter itself, with answers at the back of the book. The majority of these tasks have been written in the interactive form that students can expect to see in their real assessments

- Test Your Learning questions of varying complexity, again with answers supplied at the back of the book. The majority of these test questions have been written in the interactive form that students can expect to see in their real assessments

The Question Bank at the back contains these key features:

- Tasks corresponding to each chapter of the Text. Some tasks are designed for learning purposes, others are of assessment standard

- The AAT's sample assessment(s) and answers and further BPP practice assessments

The emphasis in all tasks and test questions is on the practical application of the skills acquired.

Supplements

From time to time we may need to publish supplementary materials to one of our titles. This can be for a variety of reasons, from a small change in the AAT unit guidance to new legislation coming into effect between editions.

You should check our supplements page regularly for anything that may affect your learning materials. All supplements are available free of charge on our supplements page on our website at:

www.bpp.com/about-bpp/aboutBPP/StudentInfo#q4

Customer feedback

If you have any comments about this book, please email nisarahmed@bpp.com or write to Nisar Ahmed, Head of Programme, BPP Learning Media Ltd, BPP House, Aldine Place, London W12 8AA.

Any feedback we receive is taken into consideration when we periodically update our materials, including comments on style, depth and coverage of AAT standards.

In addition, although our products pass through strict technical checking and quality control processes, unfortunately errors may occasionally slip through when producing material to tight deadlines.

When we learn of an error in a batch of our printed materials, either from internal review processes or from customers using our materials, we want to make sure customers are made aware of this as soon as possible and the appropriate action is taken to minimise the impact on student learning.

As a result, when we become aware of any such errors we will:

1) Include details of the error and, if necessary, PDF prints of any revised pages under the related subject heading on our 'supplements' page at: www.bpp.com/about-bpp/aboutBPP/StudentInfo#q4

2) Update the source files ahead of any further printing of the materials

3) Investigate the reason for the error and take appropriate action to minimise the risk of reoccurrence.

A NOTE ON TERMINOLOGY

The AAT AQ2013 assessments use international terminology based on International Financial Reporting Standards (IFRSs). Although you may be familiar with UK terminology, you need to now know the equivalent international terminology for your assessments.

The following information is taken from an article on the AAT's website and compares IFRS terminology with UK GAAP terminology. It then goes on to describe the impact of IFRS terminology on students studying for each level of the AAT QCF qualification.

Note that since the article containing the information below was published, there have been changes made to some IFRSs. Therefore BPP Learning Media have updated the table and other information below to reflect these changes.

In particular, the primary performance statement under IFRSs which was formerly known as the 'income statement' or the 'statement of comprehensive income' is now called the 'statement of profit or loss' or the 'statement of profit or loss and other comprehensive income'.

What is the impact of IFRS terms on AAT assessments?

The list shown in the table that follows gives the 'translation' between UK GAAP and IFRS.

UK GAAP	IFRS
Final accounts	Financial statements
Trading and profit and loss account	**Statement of profit or loss (or statement of profit or loss and other comprehensive income)**
Turnover or Sales	Revenue or Sales Revenue
Sundry income	Other operating income
Interest payable	Finance costs
Sundry expenses	Other operating costs
Operating profit	Profit from operations
Net profit/loss	Profit/Loss for the year/period
Balance sheet	**Statement of financial position**
Fixed assets	Non-current assets
Net book value	Carrying amount
Tangible assets	Property, plant and equipment

UK GAAP	IFRS
Reducing balance depreciation	Diminishing balance depreciation
Depreciation/Depreciation expense(s)	Depreciation charge(s)
Stocks	Inventories
Trade debtors or Debtors	Trade receivables
Prepayments	Other receivables
Debtors and prepayments	Trade and other receivables
Cash at bank and in hand	Cash and cash equivalents
Trade creditors or Creditors	Trade payables
Accruals	Other payables
Creditors and accruals	Trade and other payables
Long-term liabilities	Non-current liabilities
Capital and reserves	Equity (limited companies)
Profit and loss balance	Retained earnings
Minority interest	Non-controlling interest
Cash flow statement	**Statement of cash flows**

This is certainly not a comprehensive list, which would run to several pages, but it does cover the main terms that you will come across in your studies and assessments. However, you won't need to know all of these in the early stages of your studies – some of the terms will not be used until you reach Level 4. For each level of the AAT qualification, the points to bear in mind are as follows:

Level 2 Certificate in Accounting

The IFRS terms do not impact greatly at this level. Make sure you are familiar with 'receivables' (also referred to as 'trade receivables'), 'payables' (also referred to as 'trade payables'), and 'inventories'. The terms sales ledger and purchases ledger – together with their control accounts – will continue to be used. Sometimes the control accounts might be called 'trade receivables control account' and 'trade payables control account'. The other term to be aware of is 'non-current asset' – this may be used in some assessments.

Level 3 Diploma in Accounting

At this level you need to be familiar with the term 'financial statements'. The financial statements comprise a 'statement of profit or loss' (previously known as an income statement), and a 'statement of financial position'. In the statement of profit or loss the term 'revenue' or 'sales revenue' takes the place of 'sales', and 'profit for the year' replaces 'net profit'. Other terms may be used in the statement of financial position – eg 'non-current assets' and 'carrying amount'. However, specialist limited company terms are not required at this level.

Level 4 Diploma in Accounting

At Level 4 a wider range of IFRS terms is needed, and in the case of Financial statements, are already in use – particularly those relating to limited companies. Note especially that a statement of profit or loss becomes a 'statement of profit or loss and other comprehensive income'.

Note: The information above was taken from an AAT article from the 'assessment news' area of the AAT website (www.aat.org.uk). However, it has been adapted by BPP Learning Media for changes in international terminology since the article was published.

ASSESSMENT STRATEGY

Indirect Tax (ITAX) is the only tax assessment at level 3. ITAX is a 90 minute assessment. The assessment material is provided by the AAT and normally delivered online. Details of additional reference material that is available in the assessment will be provided in advance of the assessment. Alternatively, with guidance and support from training providers, learners can provide workplace evidence to be assessed locally by their training provider. The local assessor (training provider) will be required to ensure that all assessment criteria are covered.

Within the learning objectives outlined below, the AAT state that emphasis is not being placed so much on recalling information, more on awareness and understanding of how to apply it.

Note that the detailed reference material is available to access through pop-up windows during the live assessment for learners to refer to where necessary. A copy of this material is provided at the back of this text.

The **ITAX assessment (AQ2013)** consists of eight tasks.

Five short-answer tasks assess learners' knowledge of the principles of VAT and their ability to understand and interpret VAT guidance given to them. Some simple calculations are required. A number of the tasks are multiple-choice or true/false statements.

Three longer tasks will require: the preparation of certain figures for inclusion on the VAT return, completion of all seven boxes for an online VAT return from information extracted from the accounting system, including identifying the figures that are automatically calculated by the online return (for total output tax and for the net amount to be paid or reclaimed), a short piece of communication to a specified person.

For the purpose of assessment, the competency level for AAT assessment is set at 70 per cent. The level descriptor in the table below describes the ability and skills students at this level must successfully demonstrate to achieve competence.

QCF Level descriptor	Summary
	Achievement at level 3 reflects the ability to identify and use relevant understanding, methods and skills to complete tasks and address problems that, while well defined, have a measure of complexity. It includes taking responsibility for initiating and completing tasks and procedures as well as exercising autonomy and judgement within limited parameters. It also reflects awareness of different perspectives or approaches within an area of study or work.

Knowledge and understanding

- Use factual, procedural and theoretical understanding to complete tasks and address problems that, while well defined, may be complex and non-routine

- Interpret and evaluate relevant information and ideas

- Be aware of the nature of the area of study or work

- Have awareness of different perspectives or approaches within the area of study or work

Application and action

- Address problems that, while well defined, may be complex and non-routine

- Identify, select and use appropriate skills, methods and procedures

- Use appropriate investigation to inform actions

- Review how effective methods and actions have been

Autonomy and accountability

- Take responsibility for initiating and completing tasks and procedures, including, where relevant, responsibility for supervising or guiding others

- Exercise autonomy and judgement within limited parameters

AAT UNIT GUIDE (AQ2013)

Indirect Tax

Introduction

Please read this document in conjunction with the standards for the unit.

This unit is Indirect Tax, L3ITAX, and part of the accounting qualification suite provided by the Association of Accounting Technicians. There is some relation between this unit and the accounting and business tax units, however it is in principle a stand-alone unit with no requirement to study any other unit.

Successful completion of this AAT unit will result in the award of one QCF unit: Indirect Tax.

The purpose of the unit

The unit is designed to ensure that learners can enter the workplace and work to ensure their employers and their employers' clients will comply with the laws and practices of indirect taxation that are relevant to this level, as laid down by Parliament and the UK tax authority, HMRC. The assessment is designed to ensure they can do this relatively unsupervised, however some degree of self-management is required for the more involved and extensive VAT needs.

Learners will understand VAT regulations, correctly identify registration requirements, be able to extract correct information from the accounts, accurately complete VAT returns, understand VAT penalties, correct errors and communicate VAT information to relevant people. VAT is subject to specific and detailed regulations, so the learner will demonstrate they are able to seek guidance from relevant sources, process what is found and communicate this to others, plus maintain their knowledge of the related aspects of VAT.

Learning objectives

After successful completion of this unit, the learner will be able to deal with the most commonly occurring VAT issues in a business. Although some basic knowledge will be expected, the emphasis is not so much on recall as on awareness and understanding. The learner will be aware that regulations exist and change, both as a result of Finance Acts and in light of guidance from HMRC (some of which will result from decisions made within the EU), so they must know how to stay up-to-date with relevant information to ensure that the business complies with the regulations and avoids surcharges and penalties. The learner will be able to extract information from the relevant source and, using their knowledge and understanding, apply the rules to the given situations as well as changing the application when rules, practices and legislation changes.

Learners will be aware of registration requirements and the existence of a variety of schemes with different requirements to suit businesses with different needs. They will be able to calculate VAT correctly and use an accounting system to extract the figures required to complete and submit the online VAT return, including being able to verify the calculations made automatically by the online return.

They will also be aware of some special circumstances that require particular attention and be able to deal with errors and changes in the VAT rate, as well as being able to communicate on VAT issues with people inside the business.

Learning outcomes

There is one QCF unit involved, named Indirect Tax. This is divided into four learning outcomes (LOs), with each LO split into one or more assessment criteria. One LO comprises purely knowledge assessment criteria, two are purely skills, and one has a mix of knowledge and skills assessment criteria.

- LO1 Understand VAT regulations (knowledge only)

- LO2 Complete VAT returns accurately and in a timely manner (skills only)

- LO3 Understand VAT penalties and make adjustments for previous errors (knowledge and skills)

- LO4 Communicate VAT information (skills only)

Delivery guidance

Learning Outcome	Assessment Criteria	Covered in Chapter
1 Understand VAT regulations (knowledge)	1.1 Identify sources of information on VAT ■ Identify relevant sources of information on VAT and extract relevant information from them. 1.2 Explain how an organisation should interact with the relevant government agency Understand: ■ HMRC is the UK tax authority, a government body entitled to require organisations to comply with VAT regulations in relation to registration, record keeping, submission of returns and payment. ■ VAT is a tax on consumer expenditure, including knowing whether the tax falls on registered businesses or the end consumer.	**1,3,5,6**

Learning Outcome	Assessment Criteria	Covered in Chapter
	■ There are a variety of methods of interacting with the tax authority, but it is advisable to get written confirmation from HMRC about issues on which doubt may arise as to the correct treatment.	
	■ HMRC are entitled to inspect VAT records during control visits. *No further detail of control visits is expected but learners are expected to understand what records can be inspected.*	
	1.3 Explain VAT registration requirements	
	Understand:	
	■ the registration threshold and when registration becomes compulsory.	
	■ circumstances in which voluntary registration may be beneficial to the business.	
	■ some of the special schemes available for business, *this will only cover annual accounting, cash accounting and flat-rate schemes).*	
	■ circumstances when deregistration may be appropriate, and the deregistration threshold.	
	■ which records must be kept and for how long.	
	1.4 Identify the information that must be included on business documentation of VAT-registered businesses, including	
	■ Content of VAT invoices.	
	■ Simplified VAT invoices.	
	■ Invoicing for zero-rated and exempt supplies.	
	■ Tax points – basic and actual, including where payment is in advance of supply or invoice is after the supply, *but not continuous supply or goods on sale or return.*	

Learning Outcome	Assessment Criteria	Covered in Chapter
	<ul><li>The importance of tax points for determining eligibility for schemes, correct rate of VAT, and including figures on the VAT return.</li><li>Time limits for VAT invoices including the 14-day and the 30-day rules.</li><li>Rounding rules on VAT invoices, including for retailers.</li></ul>1.5 Explain the requirements and the frequency of reporting for these VAT schemes: annual accounting; cash accounting; flat-rate scheme; standard scheme<ul><li>Know the requirements of the standard scheme and the accounting schemes which can simplify a business's VAT, including the nine instalment payment regime for the annual accounting scheme but not the alternative three instalment payment method. *The VAT retail and VAT margin schemes are not required.*</li><li>Explain in broad terms the way in which each scheme works and the situations in which an organisation would be likely to use one.</li><li>Know the effect of each scheme on the frequency of VAT reporting and payments.</li></ul>1.6 Maintain an up-to-date knowledge of changes to codes of practice, regulation or legislation<ul><li>Know that information about legislation changes can be found on the HMRC and other government websites, in direct communications with businesses by HMRC, in technical circulars in accountancy firms, and in specialist journals.</li></ul>	

Learning Outcome	Assessment Criteria	Covered in Chapter
	▪ Know how to identify changes in practice by attending CPD updates, reading relevant journals and meeting other professionals. ▪ Know that changes must be applied in practice within stipulated timescales. ▪ Understand the importance of CPD in relation to keeping up-to-date with VAT.	

2 Complete VAT returns accurately and in a timely manner (skills)	2.1 Extract relevant data for a specific period from the accounting system
	
	▪ Extract relevant income, expenditure and VAT figures from the following general ledger accounts:
	  – sales and sales returns accounts
	  – purchases and purchases returns accounts
	  – cash account
	  – petty cash account
	  – VAT account
	▪ Know that figures in each of these accounts are entered from relevant books of original entry, including:
	  – sales and sales returns day books
	  – purchases and purchases returns day books
	  – cash book
	  – petty cash book
	  – journal (for errors)
	
	2.2 Calculate relevant inputs and outputs using these VAT classifications: standard supplies; exempt supplies; zero-rated supplies; imports; exports
	
	▪ Know what are inputs and outputs, and what is meant by input and output tax
	▪ Calculate correctly the input and output figures for:
	  – standard supplies
	  – exempt supplies
		2,3,4

Learning Outcome	Assessment Criteria	Covered in Chapter
	– zero-rated supplies – imports and acquisitions – exports and despatches *No knowledge required of the detail of which specific items fall into each category. No understanding of reduced rate or out of scope at this stage.*	
	▪ Know how to treat different types of inputs and outputs in preparing a VAT return, including the exclusion of pro forma invoices.	
	▪ Know in broad terms how imports and exports, and their related VAT, are treated on a VAT return, including the significance of the EU.	
	▪ Know that exports are normally zero-rated. *Candidates are not expected to have knowledge of Intrastat returns, or anything to do with point of sales of services rules, the reverse charge rules for services to EU member states or any of the procedures for digital e-services in the EU (VATMOSS).*	
	▪ Understand the effect of exempt supplies on the calculation of input and output figures.	
	▪ Recognise the implication of the difference between zero-rated and exempt supplies with respect to reclaiming input tax.	
	▪ Understand the basics of partial exemption, including an awareness of the 'de minimus limit' that enables full recovery of input tax for businesses with mixed exempt and taxable supplies. *Calculations will not be required.*	
	▪ Using the basic rounding rule, calculate correctly the VAT for standard supplies from net sales. *The detailed rounding rules based on lines of goods and services and tax per unit or article are not required.*	

Learning Outcome	Assessment Criteria	Covered in Chapter
	▪ Calculate the amount of VAT arising when given the gross amount of a supply.	
	▪ Correctly account for VAT on: employee and business entertainment, including where there is a mixed group of people being entertained (clients, employees and suppliers); sales and purchases of cars and vans; deposits or advance payments.	
	▪ Be aware of fuel scale charges, and the effect on the total VAT payable/reclaimable.	
	▪ Be aware of when bad debt relief may be available.	
	2.3 Calculate the VAT due to, or from, the relevant tax authority	
	▪ Correctly calculate VAT payable to or reclaimable from HMRC for a VAT period in respect of:	
	– Transactions in the current period including sales and purchase invoices and credits, cash payments and receipts, petty cash payments	
	– Adjustments for bad debt relief	
	– Correction of errors in previous VAT returns	
	2.4 Complete and submit a VAT return and any associated payment within the statutory time limits	
	▪ Know what the time limits are for submitting a VAT return and making payment, including those relating to special schemes.	
	▪ Complete all the relevant boxes of the online VAT return in the manner laid down by HMRC.	
	▪ Calculate the amount of VAT owing to or reclaimable from HMRC having completed the VAT return.	

Learning Outcome	Assessment Criteria	Covered in Chapter
	▪ Be aware that nearly all businesses must submit the VAT return and pay online, and that the submission dates for the return and for payment may differ depending on whether electronic funds transfer or direct debit payment is used. ▪ Understand that the balance on the VAT account should agree with the figure calculated as a result of preparing the VAT return, and provide explanations for any difference. ▪ Understand the basics of the process for reclaiming VAT from HMRC.	

3 Understand VAT penalties and make adjustments for previous errors	3.1 Explain the implications and penalties for an organisation resulting from failure to abide by VAT regulations (knowledge)
	
	▪ Know the consequences of late submission of VAT returns.
	
	▪ Know the main principles of the enforcement regime:
	
	    – Know what triggers a surcharge liability notice and that a default surcharge may be payable if a further default arises in the surcharge period; *learners will not be expected to know how the amount of the default surcharge is calculated*
	
	    – know that an HMRC assessment may be raised if no VAT return is submitted
	
	    – know that penalties may be payable for errors, inaccurate returns and late registration
	
	    – know that evasion of VAT is a criminal offence
		6

Learning Outcome	Assessment Criteria	Covered in Chapter
	3.2 Make adjustments and declarations for any errors or omissions identified in previous VAT periods (skills) ■ Identify whether the error or omission in the amount of VAT due to or reclaimable from HMRC can be adjusted on the current VAT return, by identifying that it falls below the threshold at which errors or omissions must be declared and within the timescale during which adjustments can be made. ■ Identify that an error or omission in the amount of VAT due to or reclaimable from HMRC can be separately declared to HMRC rather than adjusted on the current VAT return. ■ Make appropriate adjustments on the VAT return for errors and omissions in the amount of VAT due to or reclaimable from HMRC. ■ Declare to HMRC an error or omission that cannot be adjusted on the current VAT return. *The nature and amount of the errors or omissions will be given.*	
4 Communicate VAT information (skills)	4.1 Inform managers of the impact that the VAT payment may have on an organisation's cash flow and financial forecasts ■ Apply the time limits within which the VAT return must be completed and payment must be made under various schemes in the context of the particular organisation and its policies. ■ Communicate this via email or memo. ■ Communicate the effect of the VAT return resulting in a reclaim from HMRC.	6

Learning Outcome	Assessment Criteria	Covered in Chapter
	4.2 Advise relevant people of changes in VAT legislation which would have an effect on an organisation's recording systems ■ Understand the implication of a change in the standard VAT rate on the organisation in terms of systems, cash flow and administration. ■ Understand who would need to be informed of changes in VAT legislation and why. ■ Advise relevant people by email or memo.	

Task	Learning outcome	Assessment criteria	Max marks	Title for topics within task range	Chapter reference
1	1	LO1.1 LO1.2 LO1.3	5	Finding out about VAT, registration, VAT records	1, 3
2	1, 2	LO1.4 LO2.2	7	VAT invoices, tax point, making exempt supplies	1, 2, 3
3	1, 2	LO1.5 LO2.2 LO2.4	5	VAT schemes, due dates, bad debt relief	3, 4, 5
4	1, 2, 3	LO1.6 LO2.2 LO3.1 LO3.2	7	Detailed VAT rules, surcharges, penalties, corrections	2, 6
5	1, 2	LO1.4 LO2.1 LO2.2 LO2.3 LO2.4	6	VAT calculations and reconciliations	2, 3, 4

Task	Learning outcome	Assessment criteria	Max marks	Title for topics within task range	Chapter reference
6	2	LO2.1 LO2.2 LO2.3 LO2.4	6	Preparing specific figures for the VAT return	4
7	2	LO2.1 LO2.2 LO2.4	17	Completing and submitting a VAT return accurately	4
8	2, 4	LO2.4 LO4.1 LO4.2	7	Communicating VAT information	4, 6

chapter 1:
VAT BASICS

chapter coverage 📖

Although you will have come across Value Added Tax (VAT) in your earlier studies, we begin with a reminder of the basics and how the VAT system works. We then start to consider the rules governing VAT, starting with registration. The topics covered in this chapter are:

✎ Basic principles

✎ The scope of VAT

✎ Registration and deregistration

  – Compulsory registration

  – Voluntary registration

  – Voluntary deregistration

BASIC PRINCIPLES

What is VAT?

Value Added Tax (VAT) is essentially a sales tax – it is a tax on consumer expenditure and is an important source of revenue for the government. The basic principle is that VAT should normally be borne by the final consumer.

VAT is an indirect tax that is collected by traders (acting as agents) in the course of their business, and paid over to HM Revenue & Customs (HMRC).

HMRC is the administering government body that requires organisations to comply with the VAT regulations which are contained in legislation.

Assessment focus:

In the live assessment you will be provided with detailed reference material outlining VAT regulations covered within this syllabus. During the assessment this reference material can be accessed through pop-up windows. A copy is included at the back of this text. Make sure you familiarise yourself with the content and practise referring to it as you work through the text and question bank.

The operation of VAT

If the sales of a business exceed a certain limit for a year, the business:

- Must register for VAT, and
- Include its VAT registration number on invoices issued.

A VAT-registered trader will:

- Charge their customers VAT – known as OUTPUT TAX or OUTPUT VAT
- Reclaim VAT on purchases – known as INPUT TAX or INPUT VAT, and
- Complete a VAT return (usually every three months).

On the VAT return, the input tax suffered is deducted from the output tax charged and the net amount paid to HMRC.

HOW IT WORKS

Let's follow a simple example through the VAT payment process.

A forester sells wood to a furniture maker for £100 plus VAT. The furniture maker uses this wood to make a table and sells the table to a shop for £150 plus VAT. The shop sells the table to the final consumer for £300 plus VAT. VAT at 20% will be accounted for to HMRC as follows.

	Cost	Input tax 20%	Net sale price	Output tax 20%	Payable to HMRC
	£	£	£	£	£
Forester	0	0	100	20	20
Furniture maker	100	20	150	30	10
Shop	150	30	300	60	30
					60

In the above example, the furniture maker has charged £30 of output tax and suffered £20 of input tax. He must pay the net amount of output tax less input tax over to HMRC, ie £10.

Note that it is usually the final customer (consumer) – often a member of the general public – who suffers the cost of the VAT.

Task 1

Business A sells goods to Business B for £1,000 plus £200 of VAT. Which business treats the VAT as input tax and which treats it as output tax?

	Input tax ✓	Output tax ✓
Business A		
Business B		

THE SCOPE OF VAT

Introduction

VAT is chargeable on TAXABLE SUPPLIES of goods and services made in the UK by TAXABLE PERSONS in the course of their business.

Taxable persons

A taxable person is a person who is, or is required to be, registered for VAT.

The term 'person' includes both individuals and companies.

Types of supply

Each supply by a trader must be categorised as either:

- A **taxable supply**, which is either standard-rated, a reduced rate supply, or zero-rated (see below)

- An **exempt supply**, which is not chargeable to VAT, or

- **'Outside the scope'** of VAT, which has no effect for VAT and the item does not need to be reported on the VAT return. Examples include dividends and the payment of wages.

  No understanding of 'reduced rate' or 'outside the scope' is needed for this assessment.

If a supplier **only makes exempt supplies** then they **CANNOT register for VAT**.

Taxable supplies

A trader making taxable supplies can, or in some circumstances must, register for VAT. Once registered, the trader must charge VAT (output tax) on his supplies at the relevant rate, but as a result can reclaim VAT (input tax) on his purchases and expenses.

There are three rates of VAT in the UK:

- STANDARD RATE 20%. The vast majority of supplies of goods and services are standard-rated. A supply should be treated as standard-rated, ie charged VAT at 20%, unless it specifically fits into one of the other categories.

- REDUCED RATE 5%. A reduced rate of VAT (5%) applies to certain supplies such as domestic fuel and power. You do not need any understanding of this reduced rate for your assessment.

- ZERO RATE 0%. Zero-rated supplies are supplies of goods and services which are technically taxable but the law states that the rate of VAT on these goods is 0%. The main reason for this is that these zero-rated supplies are normally essential items which, if they were taxed, would be an additional burden to the less well-off.

Assessment focus:

No knowledge is required of the detail of which specific items fall into each category of standard, exempt and zero-rated. You will not therefore have to decide whether a particular item is, for example standard-rated or zero-rated, just understand how the different categories are treated.

The effect on a business which makes zero-rated supplies is that although it is allowed to VAT register, it will charge output VAT at 0% on its sales but can

reclaim any input VAT on its purchases. Therefore, for example, a VAT-registered bus company charges no VAT on its fares (as travel is zero-rated) but it is able to reclaim from HMRC any VAT on its purchases and expenses such as fuel and service costs. So the cost to the bus company of its purchases and expenses is the **VAT-exclusive** amount.

The difference between exempt supplies and zero-rated supplies is that if a supplier makes only exempt supplies then it cannot register for VAT and therefore cannot reclaim the input VAT on any of its purchases and expenses. As a result, the costs of purchases and expenses to such a supplier is the **VAT-inclusive** amount.

Task 2

The following businesses have just paid telephone bills of £1,200 (£1,000 plus VAT of £200).

What is the net cost incurred by each business in relation to the telephone bills?

Business type	Type of supply made	Net cost £
Insurance company	Only exempt supplies	
Accountancy firm	Only standard-rated supplies	
Bus company	Only zero-rated supplies	

REGISTRATION AND DEREGISTRATION

Introduction

A business that makes **taxable supplies** may **choose** or may **be required** to register for VAT.

As already mentioned, once registered, a trader must charge output tax on his supplies at the relevant rate, but as a result can reclaim input tax on his purchases and expenses.

If registration is compulsory, **late registration penalties can apply if registration is not made on time** (see Chapter 6).

Compulsory registration

A person making taxable supplies **must** register for VAT **within 30 days** if:

- At the end of any month, **taxable turnover** (excluding VAT) in the previous twelve months (or the period since the business started, if shorter) exceeds the registration threshold of £82,000 (historical test), or

A person making taxable supplies **must** register for VAT **without delay** if:

- At any time, **taxable turnover** (excluding VAT) in the next 30 days *alone* is expected to exceed the registration threshold of £82,000 (future test).

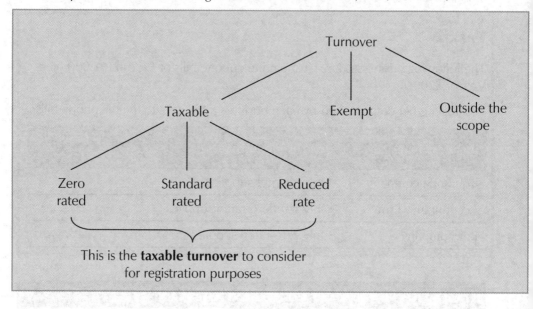

This is the **taxable turnover** to consider for registration purposes

HOW IT WORKS – HISTORIC TEST

Jack started in business on 1 July 2015. His monthly VAT-exclusive turnover is:

	£
Standard-rated supplies	7,000
Zero-rated supplies	2,850
Exempt supplies	600
TOTAL	10,450

1. Calculate the VAT exclusive taxable turnover for each month (standard plus zero-rated supplies). Exclude the exempt supplies.

   Taxable turnover is £9,850 per month (£7,000 + £2,850)

2. Work out when the £82,000 registration limit is exceeded (if at all), up to a maximum of a 12 month period.

   After eight months (28 February 2016) cumulative turnover is £78,800, so the limit is not exceeded.

   After nine months (31 March 2016) cumulative turnover is £88,650 so the limit is exceeded.

   Therefore after nine months, Jack must register for VAT within 30 days (ie by 30 April 2016).

Under the historic test, non-registered traders must review their taxable turnover at the end of every calendar month to ensure that they have not exceeded the registration threshold.

HOW IT WORKS – FUTURE TEST

Orla has been in business for many years with VAT-exclusive turnover of approximately £6,500 per month (£78,000 per annum) and so has not yet had to register under the historic test. On 24 November 2015, Orla won a major contract which will immediately bring in additional income of approximately £78,500 per month.

Taxable turnover in the next 30 days alone will be £85,000 (£6,500 + £78,500), which exceeds the threshold, therefore Orla must register for VAT without delay.

Task 3

Amy started trading on 1 August 2015. Her monthly sales (excluding VAT) are:

	£
Standard-rated supplies	7,850
Zero-rated supplies	1,270
Exempt supplies	700
	9,820

By what date will Amy exceed the threshold for VAT?

By what date must Amy register for VAT?

Task 4

Richard made taxable supplies of £72,000 in his first 11 months of trading. His taxable supplies in month 12 are £11,000.

Which of the following explains why Richard must register for VAT? Tick ONE box.

	✓
At the beginning of month 12, Richard expects his taxable supplies will exceed £82,000 in the next 30 days.	
At the end of month 12, Richard's taxable supplies in the previous 12 months have exceeded £82,000.	

Voluntary registration

If a business's taxable turnover is below the annual registration limit it is still possible for the business to register for VAT on a voluntary basis.

The main advantage of voluntary registration is the ability to recover input tax.

In particular, if a business makes zero-rated supplies then it may be advantageous to register for VAT

- Output VAT at 0% (ie nil) has to be charged on its sales but
- It can reclaim the input VAT on its purchases and expenses.

Therefore the business is in a net cash repayment position.

Some businesses may want to VAT register to improve the image of the business. However the disadvantages include:

- The administrative burden of preparing regular VAT returns,

- The potential for incurring penalties, and

- Loss of business from non-registered customers if prices increase by the output tax.

Task 5

Decide why a business making taxable supplies might choose to register for VAT voluntarily. Tick ONE box.

	✓
Preparation of VAT returns would be optional	
Customers would benefit by being able to claim back input VAT	
Business would benefit by being able to claim back input VAT	

Exemption from registration if mainly zero-rated supplies

A trader making only (or mainly) zero-rated supplies can apply to HMRC to be exempt from registering for VAT.

This means the trader would not be able to reclaim input tax suffered, but would eliminate the administrative burden of preparing VAT returns. It may therefore suit traders that pay little or no VAT on purchases and expenses.

Registration decision tree

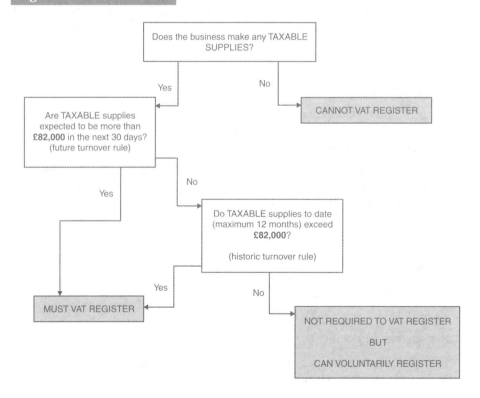

Voluntary deregistration

A VAT-registered business may find that its taxable turnover falls or is expected to fall.

If the taxable turnover for the previous 12 months is equal to or below the deregistration limit of £80,000, or in the next 12 months is expected to fall beneath the deregistration limit, then the business can apply to HMRC to deregister.

VAT cannot be charged on any supplies from the date of deregistration.

Exception from registration if temporarily exceed threshold

A trader can apply for exception from registration if:

- The trader should register because the value of his taxable supplies in the previous 12 months have exceeded the registration threshold of £82,000 (ie the historic test is met) *but*

- The trader can demonstrate to HMRC that in the longer term he will only be trading below the deregistration threshold of £80,000, ie he has only exceeded the registration threshold temporarily.

The trader needs to write a letter to HMRC, explaining why his taxable supplies will not go over the deregistration threshold in the next 12 months. If HMRC does not agree to make an exception, the trader will become registered for VAT from the day he should have been registered and will need to account for VAT from that date.

Assessment focus

Don't forget, much of the information covered in this chapter is available to view throughout the live assessment within the detailed reference material. Therefore you don't need to memorise all the facts.

Apart from basic knowledge, the emphasis at this level is not so much on recall of information, but instead on awareness that regulations exist, know how to find that information, and apply it correctly to given scenarios.

Turn to the reference material at the back of the text and try to identify the areas covered within this chapter.

They include:

- Introduction to VAT

- Rates of VAT

- Registration and deregistration limits

- Exempt and partly-exempt businesses (we look at partly-exempt businesses in the next chapter of this text)

The information included in this chapter will typically be tested in the following tasks:

Task 1 **Finding out about VAT, registration,** VAT records

Task 2 VAT invoices, tax point, **making exempt supplies**

Performance feedback

The assessor's recent comments relevant to this chapter can be summarised as follows:

Of great concern is the general lack of knowledge of the basic registration and deregistration rules for VAT. This is particularly noticeable when "zero-rated" supplies are included in the task and many students fail to include the value of these in the total amount of taxable supplies for registration.

Given that registration failures are one of the biggest areas for penalties for small businesses it follows that this is an area which requires more detailed tuition and learning.

It is clear that in some cases students are not reading questions carefully enough. Take for example a task which asks about who bears the cost of the VAT added to the selling price of a product. Clearly if the final purchaser of the product is a member of the public then any option which states that this is the person who "suffers" the tax will be the correct one, however if any other person in the chain of events is not registered then the final outcome may change completely.

With different options to consider, each of them a valid answer in certain circumstances, students need to read both the task and each of the options carefully and it is important to read the task and then apply each answer to it individually to check which one fits best. If this process is rushed then there is a risk that an inappropriate option will be selected in haste.

CHAPTER OVERVIEW

- VAT is an indirect tax administered by HM Revenue and Customs.
- A purchaser who is not VAT registered bears the cost of the VAT. This is normally the final purchaser in the supply chain who is often a member of the public.
- There are three types of supply – taxable supplies, exempt supplies and supplies that are outside the scope of VAT.
- In the UK there are three rates of VAT for taxable supplies – the standard rate of 20%, a reduced rate of 5% for certain supplies such as domestic fuel and power, and the zero rate.
- In a VAT-registered business, VAT does not increase the selling prices of either zero-rated supplies or exempt supplies – however if a business makes exempt supplies it cannot reclaim the input tax on its purchases and expenses – if the supplies made by the business are zero-rated then input VAT can be reclaimed.
- The cost of purchases to a VAT-registered business making taxable supplies is generally the VAT-exclusive price. The cost of purchases to a business not registered for VAT, including a business making wholly exempt supplies, is the VAT-inclusive price.
- When a business's taxable turnover reaches the registration limit then the business must register for VAT, otherwise the business is liable for penalties.
- Some businesses may find it advantageous to register for VAT although the registration limit has not been met – this is known as voluntary registration.
- If a business's taxable turnover falls below the deregistration limit then the business can apply to HMRC to deregister.

Keywords

Output VAT or Output tax – VAT on the sale of goods and the provision of services. This is paid by the business to HMRC

Input VAT or Input tax – VAT on the purchases of goods and payment of expenses. This is reclaimed by the business from HMRC

Exempt supplies – supplies on which no VAT is charged

Standard-rated supplies – goods and services which are taxable at a rate of 20%

Zero-rated supplies – goods and services which are taxable but the rate of tax on them is 0%

Taxable turnover – this includes standard-rated, reduced rate and zero-rated sales, but excludes exempt sales

Registration – the process required if a business making taxable supplies must, (if it exceeds the registration limits) or wants to, start charging (and recovering) VAT. VAT must be charged on taxable supplies from the date of registration

Deregistration – the process required to end a registration. VAT cannot be charged on any supplies from the date of deregistration

TEST YOUR LEARNING

Test 1

Which organisation administers VAT in the UK? Tick the relevant box below.

	✓
HM Customs & Excise	
Inland Revenue	
HM Revenue & Customs	
HM Treasury	

Test 2

Choose which ONE of the following statements is correct. Tick the relevant box below.

	✓
Output VAT is the VAT charged by a supplier on the sales that are made by his business. Output VAT is collected by the supplier and paid over to HMRC.	
Output VAT is the VAT suffered by the purchaser of the goods which will be reclaimed from HMRC if the purchaser is VAT registered.	

Test 3

Explain how it is normally the final consumer that pays the full amount of VAT to the seller but never pays any money to HMRC.

Test 4

Identify whether the following statements are True or False.

	True ✓	False ✓
If a business supplies zero-rated services then the business is not able to reclaim the VAT on its purchases and expenses from HMRC.		
A business makes zero-rated supplies. The cost to the business of its purchases and expenses is the VAT exclusive amount.		

Test 5

The following three businesses are trying to decide whether they need to register for VAT immediately, within the next 30 days, or whether they just need to monitor the situation for the time being. Tick the correct box for each line.

		Register without delay	Register within 30 days	Monitor and register later
A	An existing business with total turnover for the previous 11 months of £80,000. Sales for the next month are unknown at present.			
B	A new business with an expected turnover for the next 12 months of £6,950 per month.			
C	An existing business with total turnover for the previous 12 months of £6,900 per month.			

Test 6

You have been contacted by a potential new client, Mrs Quirke. She has recently started trading as an interior designer.

By selecting from the options listed, complete the following letter to her explaining when her business must register for VAT.

AN Accountant
Number Street
London
SW11 8AB

Mrs Quirke
Alphabet Street
London
W12 6WM

Dear Mrs Quirke

VAT REGISTRATION

Further to our recent telephone conversation, set out below are the circumstances when you must register your business for VAT.

If the taxable turnover of your business at the end of a month, looking back no more than (1) [____ ▼] months, has exceeded the registration limit of (2) £ [____ ▼] then the business must apply to register for VAT within 30 days.

Alternatively, if at any time, the taxable turnover (before any VAT is added) is expected to exceed the registration limit within the next (3) [____ ▼] alone then the business must apply to be registered for VAT without delay. This would be the situation if, for example, you obtained a large additional contract for, say, £85,000.

If you wish to discuss this in any more detail please do not hesitate to contact me.

Yours sincerely

AN Accountant

Picklist:

(1) six / 12 / 24

(2) £80,000 / £82,000

(3) week / 30 days / 12 months

chapter 2:
INPUTS AND OUTPUTS

CALCULATION OF VAT

Introduction

As mentioned in Chapter 1, once VAT-registered, a trader must charge output tax on his taxable supplies at the relevant rate.

VAT is charged on taxable supplies on the **VAT exclusive** or **'net'** value. Sometimes however, the VAT inclusive or 'gross' price may be given, for example, on less detailed or simplified VAT invoices (see Chapter 3).

Therefore you need to be able to calculate the correct amount of VAT from both VAT inclusive (gross) and VAT exclusive (net) figures.

Calculating the VAT

For standard-rated supplies the VAT is charged at 20%.

Type of supply	Apply to 'net' value (VAT exclusive)	Apply to 'gross' value (VAT inclusive)
Standard-rated supply	20%	1/6 (20/120)

HOW IT WORKS

An invoice shows a total VAT inclusive (gross) amount of £48.00. The amount of VAT at 20% included in this amount can be calculated as follows:

£48.00 × 20/120 = £8.00

or

£48.00 × 1/6 = £8.00

You can check this working by applying the 20% to the VAT exclusive (net) amount:

£48.00 less £8.00 (VAT worked out above) = £40.00 (net amount)

£40.00 × 20% = £8.00

Task 1

Complete the following table.

Net £	VAT rate %	VAT £	Gross £
	20		52.20
18.00	20		

The calculation of VAT in situations where a discount is offered is covered in Chapter 3, when we look at VAT invoices.

Rounding of VAT

The total VAT on an invoice should be rounded **down** to the nearest penny, and this is generally the treatment you should use when calculating VAT in the assessment.

RECLAIMING INPUT TAX

A VAT-registered trader who makes taxable supplies (ie zero, reduced or standard-rated) can reclaim the input tax it incurs on:

- Goods and services purchased from another taxable 'person'
- Goods **imported** from non-EU countries (see section 4 below), and
- **Acquisitions** from EU member states (see section 4 below).

Input tax is recoverable from HMRC, either by deducting it from output tax charged, or by claiming a repayment, on the VAT return. The trader will only be able to recover the input tax if he has a valid VAT invoice, which we will see in Chapter 3.

Cost to the business

In Chapter 1 we learnt that if a trader **makes only exempt supplies** and so cannot register for VAT and cannot reclaim input tax, the cost of purchases to such a trader is the **VAT-inclusive (gross) amount**.

Usually (when input tax is recoverable), the cost to a VAT-registered business of buying goods and services is the **VAT-exclusive (net) amount**. For example:

	£
Amount paid to supplier (VAT-inclusive)	1,200
Input VAT reclaimed from HMRC	(200)
Net cost to the business (VAT-exclusive)	1,000

However in certain circumstances, a business may not be able to recover all the input tax it has incurred on its purchases. Where VAT is irrecoverable (as we will see below) the cost to the business is the **VAT-inclusive amount.**

Business entertaining

A business cannot reclaim input tax incurred on most business entertaining expenses. However, the input VAT on entertaining overseas customers (not UK or Isle of Man) and entertaining staff can be reclaimed.

Business entertaining includes free or subsidised entertainment or hospitality to anyone who is not an employee.

If a business entertains both employees and non-employees, the input VAT needs to be apportioned, and only that relating to employees can be reclaimed. Therefore, if a business spends £500 plus £100 VAT on a Christmas party for 60 employees and 40 UK customers, only the VAT in relation to entertaining employees (£60) is recoverable. The cost of the party to the business is £540, being £500 plus £40 irrecoverable VAT.

Cars and vans

The distinction between capital and revenue does not apply for VAT. For example if plant (subject to VAT) is bought for use in a VAT-registered business, the input tax can be reclaimed, as long as the plant is used to make taxable supplies.

However, when purchasing a car (eg company cars for sales people etc), including accessories fitted when purchased and delivery charges, **VAT cannot be reclaimed.** There are some exceptions to this, for example cars used:

- Exclusively for business purposes (eg pool cars),
- Within a taxi business,
- For driving instruction, or
- Within a self-drive hire business.

If VAT is **not reclaimed on the original purchase** of a new car, no VAT is charged on the subsequent sale. **The sale will be exempt** for VAT purposes.

However if input tax was recoverable (eg on a taxi) output tax must be charged when the car is sold.

Note that **VAT is generally recoverable on the purchase of a commercial vehicle such as a van.**

The summary table below shows how input tax and output tax applies to the purchase and sale of certain vehicles.

Capital item	Input tax recoverable on purchase?	Output tax chargeable on sale of item?
New car for salesman	NO	NO - Exempt
Car used in taxi business	YES	YES
Van	YES	YES

Task 2

Identify whether input tax can be reclaimed by a VAT-registered business in each of the following circumstances.

Circumstance	Yes, can reclaim ✓	No, cannot reclaim ✓
Input tax incurred entertaining prospective new UK client		
Input tax incurred on a new car for the top salesperson		
Input tax incurred on a car for use in a driving instruction business		

VAT on Road Fuel

Where a business purchases fuel for cars and retains a VAT invoice, it can reclaim the input VAT on that fuel, **providing the fuel is only used for business journeys.**

When there is **private use** of a car and fuel is provided, any of the following arrangements can be put in place regarding the fuel:

- Keep sufficiently detailed mileage records and reclaim input tax only on the fuel purchased for business journeys.

- Reclaim all the input tax, and pay an amount of output tax, the appropriate FUEL SCALE CHARGE, to account for private use of the car (see below).

- Agree not to reclaim any input tax in respect of road fuel purchased by the business for any (including commercial) vehicle.

With the **fuel scale charge** system, all of the input VAT can be reclaimed on the purchase of the fuel regardless of whether the fuel is used for business or private purposes. However, an amount of output tax must also be paid over to HMRC to account for the private use. This output tax is known as the fuel scale charge and the amount charged is based on the CO_2 emissions of the vehicle.

Fuel scale charges can be looked up in tables, for example on the HMRC website, but while you have to understand when they apply, you do not have to be able to calculate them.

The fuel scale charge will increase the amount **payable** to HMRC.

Task 3

Decide whether each of the following statements is True or False.

	True ✓	False ✓
A VAT-registered business can reclaim all the input VAT on road fuel if it keeps detailed records of business and private mileage, and makes no other adjustment.		
A VAT-registered business can reclaim all the input VAT on road fuel if it pays the appropriate fuel scale charge for private mileage.		

PARTIAL EXEMPTION

Basic principles

Remember all supplies must fit into one of three categories:

- Taxable supplies
- Exempt supplies
- Outside the scope of VAT (although no understanding is needed of this)

Taxable supplies are further categorised as follows:

- Standard-rated – charge output tax at 20%

- Reduced rate – charge output tax at 5% (although no understanding is needed of this)

- Zero-rated – charge output tax at 0%

We know that traders making only taxable supplies can or must register for VAT and consequently recover their input tax on expenses, and those making only exempt supplies cannot register and so cannot recover their input tax.

Some traders, however may make both taxable and exempt supplies and will be classed as **partially exempt** traders.

Attributing input tax

For a trader who is partially exempt, some of his purchases and expenses are incurred in making or selling taxable supplies, and some purchases and expenses are incurred making or selling exempt supplies. Some purchases and expenses may relate to both types of supply. Therefore, the input tax on purchases and expenses must be categorised between that relating to taxable supplies and that relating to exempt supplies, in order to decide how much input tax is recoverable.

Where a trader is partially exempt he is generally only able to recover the input tax on supplies made to him that is **attributable to his taxable supplies**.

However, if the input tax incurred relating to EXEMPT supplies is below a **de minimis** amount then all input VAT can be recovered in full.

Task 4

Decide whether each of the following statements is True or False.

	True ✓	False ✓
A VAT-registered business can reclaim all the input VAT attributed to zero-rated supplies		
A VAT-registered business can reclaim all the input VAT attributed to standard-rated supplies		
A VAT-registered business can reclaim all the input VAT attributed to exempt supplies		
A VAT-registered business can reclaim all the input VAT attributed to both taxable and exempt supplies providing certain de minimis tests are satisfied		

OVERSEAS TRANSACTIONS

Introduction

The treatment of VAT on transactions with countries outside the UK depends upon whether the other country is within the European Union (EU) or outside it.

Purchases of goods from other countries can be categorised as follows:

- IMPORTS – goods purchased from a country outside the EU.

- ACQUISITIONS – goods purchased from another country within the EU.

Goods **sold** to other countries can be categorised as follows:

- EXPORTS – goods sold to a country outside the EU.

- DESPATCHES – goods sold to a country within the EU.

We look at each situation in turn.

Imports

If goods are purchased from a country outside the EU the following treatment is required for VAT:

- The VAT is normally deemed to be at the same rate as on a supply of the same goods in the UK. This VAT is usually paid by the customer to HMRC as the goods enter the UK (ie at the port or the airport).

- The VAT paid at the port/airport is then reclaimed as input tax on the VAT return.

The net effect is the same as buying from a UK supplier:

- Buying from a UK supplier, the customer pays the VAT to the supplier (as part of the invoice total), then reclaims the input VAT from HMRC on the VAT return.

- Buying from outside the EU, the customer pays the VAT to HMRC at the port or airport, then reclaims the input VAT from HMRC on the VAT return.

Acquisitions

If goods are purchased by a UK buyer from a VAT-registered business in another EU country, and the goods are sent to the UK, the EU supplier will not charge VAT (and neither will HMRC at the ports/airports).

Instead, the UK purchaser must **charge himself the VAT due on those goods on his VAT return**. This VAT can be treated as input tax as well as being an amount of output tax due to HMRC.

Again the net effect is the same as above BUT no cash changes hands.

- Buying from a supplier in another EU country the customer 'pays' output tax to HMRC on the VAT return, then 'reclaims' the input VAT from HMRC on the same VAT return (net effect nil unless partially exempt as above).

Exports

Goods exported to any country outside the EU are normally treated as **zero-rated supplies** provided that there is documentary evidence of the export and that this is obtained by the supplier within three months of the supply.

Despatches

If goods are sold to an EU customer there are two different scenarios:

- If the EU customer is a **VAT-registered business** in the EU country he will be charged VAT at the ZERO rate. To benefit from zero rating, the customer must provide his **EU VAT-registration number** (which is then shown on the invoice). Additionally the VAT registration numbers of both the supplier and customer must include the EU country code (for example GB).

- If the customer is **not EU VAT-registered** (or his EU VAT registration number has not been given) then UK VAT is charged as if a normal UK sale (ie STANDARD rate in most cases).

Later in the Text we will see how these transactions are entered onto the VAT return.

Task 5

A UK VAT-registered trader sells goods to both VAT-registered and non VAT-registered traders elsewhere in the EU. If these goods had been sold in the UK they would have been standard-rated. Which of the following is the correct treatment assuming all other conditions are fulfilled? Tick ONE box.

To VAT-registered traders	To non VAT-registered traders	✓
Zero-rated	Zero-rated	
Standard-rated	Zero-rated	
Zero-rated	Standard-rated	
Standard-rated	Standard-rated	

Task 6

Joe, a VAT-registered trader, acquires goods from a VAT-registered supplier in another EU country. Tick the box that describes how Joe should deal with this acquisition for VAT.

	✓
No VAT is charged by the EU supplier therefore can be ignored by Joe on his VAT return	
Joe must pay output VAT to HMRC at the port/airport and can reclaim input VAT on the next return	
Joe must charge himself 'output VAT' and 'reclaim input' VAT on the same return	

Assessment focus:

Don't forget, much of the information covered in this chapter is available to view throughout the live assessment within the detailed reference material. Turn to the back of the Text and try to identify the areas covered within this chapter.

They include:

- *Exempt and partly-exempt businesses*
- *Entertainment expenses*
- *Vehicles and motoring expenses*
- *Transactions outside the UK*

The information included in this chapter will typically be tested in the following tasks:

*Task 2 VAT invoices, tax point, **making exempt supplies***

*Task 4 **Detailed VAT rules,** surcharges, penalties, corrections*

*Task 5 **VAT calculations** and reconciliations*

Performance feedback

The assessor's recent comments relevant to this chapter can be summarised as follows:

Of particular concern is the knowledge of zero-rated and partial exempt VAT situations. This appears to be a common issue for students who fail to identify the input tax recovery rules for either of these situations.

Additional concern is the approach to VAT on special cases (of recovering input tax) where there is a general failure to understand the special calculations needed

when a business works within these areas (tasks could pose questions on any of them from retail to car hire business and on acquisitions and despatches from and to other member states). In many cases students feel VAT is chargeable when it is not, and reclaimable, or not reclaimable when in fact the opposite is true.

Routine calculation of VAT is fine, students tend to do well on this.

CHAPTER OVERVIEW

- VAT is charged on standard-rated supplies at 20%. Therefore, the VAT amount in a VAT-inclusive price is found by multiplying by 1/6.

- The VAT on business entertainment expenses of UK customers and (usually) on the purchase of cars for use within a business is non-reclaimable.

- If input VAT is reclaimed on fuel used for private journeys, an amount of output VAT (the fuel scale charge) also has to be charged.

- If a VAT-registered business makes both taxable and exempt supplies the recovery of input tax will be restricted, subject to the de minimis limits.

- Goods imported from outside the EU are normally deemed to be charged at the same rate as goods in the UK.

- The VAT on acquisitions of goods from other EU countries is treated as both output tax and input tax.

- Exports of goods to another country outside the EU are normally treated as zero-rated supplies.

- Despatches of goods to other EU countries are usually zero-rated if the customer is VAT-registered, and has provided his VAT-registration number. Otherwise, they are treated as if they were normal UK sales.

Keywords

Fuel scale charge – an output VAT charge to offset against the input VAT reclaimed on fuel purchased for private use

Partial exemption – when a business makes a mixture of taxable and exempt supplies then input VAT attributable to exempt supplies may only be reclaimed subject to satisfying de minimis tests

Imports – goods purchased from a country outside the European Union

Exports – goods sold to a country outside the European Union

Acquisitions – goods purchased from another European Union country

Despatches – goods sold to another European Union country

TEST YOUR LEARNING

Test 1

Business C sells goods to Business D for £384.00 plus the standard rate of VAT. Both businesses are VAT-registered.

(a)

The VAT is £	

(b) **Which business will treat it as output tax and which will treat it as input tax?**

	Output tax ✓	Input tax ✓
Business C		
Business D		

Test 2

Identify which TWO of the following types of expenditure have irrecoverable input tax.

	✓
Staff party	
Car for sales manager	
Photocopier	
Entertaining UK clients	

Test 3

You have received four invoices from suppliers which show only the total VAT-inclusive price and the fact that all of the goods are standard-rated. For each invoice total determine the amount of VAT that is included.

Complete the following table.

VAT-inclusive £	VAT at 20 % £
42.88	
96.57	
28.20	
81.07	

Test 4

A UK VAT-registered business is exporting goods which are standard-rated in the UK to an American business. **Which ONE of the following statements is correct? Tick the relevant box.**

	✓
The goods will be treated as standard-rated in the UK if the American business is VAT-registered.	
The goods will be treated as standard-rated in the UK provided documentary evidence of the export is obtained within three months.	
The goods will be treated as zero-rated in the UK if the American business is VAT-registered.	
The goods will be treated as zero-rated in the UK provided documentary evidence of the export is obtained within three months.	

chapter 3:
ACCOUNTING FOR VAT

chapter coverage 📖

In this chapter we focus on the records a VAT-registered trader must keep and the detail to be included on various types for VAT invoice. We also look at how a business decides which tax period to include a transaction in and when a trader can claim bad debt relief on an unpaid invoice. The topics covered are:

- ✍ Keeping records
- ✍ VAT invoices
- ✍ Credit notes and debit notes
- ✍ Tax point
- ✍ Bad debt relief

KEEPING RECORDS

Introduction

HMRC sets out in detail the records that should be kept by a VAT-registered business.

It is important that **records exist of all transactions**. This is essential since traders may be claiming refunds of input tax and HMRC may wish to verify that the tax has, in fact, been paid. The trader must also properly account for output tax that has been collected and HMRC may wish to verify this.

Each individual business accounting system will be different but, in general terms, you must keep **records of all standard-rated, reduced rate, zero-rated and exempt goods and services which you receive or supply.**

The records must be complete and kept up-to-date in order that, each quarter, the correct amount of VAT due to or from HMRC can be calculated and entered onto the VAT return.

Whatever method the business uses to keep these records, they must be kept in such a way that HMRC officers can easily check that the figures on the VAT returns are correct.

Information that must be recorded

A VAT-registered trader must keep and preserve the following business and VAT records:

- Business and accounting records (including journals)

- Copies of all tax invoices issued

- Tax invoices received

- Documentation relating to his imports and exports, and EU acquisitions and despatches of goods

- All credit notes and debit notes received

- Copies of all credit notes and debit notes issued

- A VAT account summarising total output and input tax for each period (see Chapter 4)

HMRC requires that these records should normally be kept for **six years**.

HMRC has an entitlement to inspect a taxpayer's VAT records at any time.

Sales records for output tax

The **input and output tax figures on the VAT return must be supported by the original or copy tax invoices**, and **certain other records.** These are not submitted with the VAT return, but must be kept in the event that HMRC wishes to inspect them.

To verify **output tax**, records should include:

- Orders and delivery notes
- Sales invoices issued. An exception to this is when less detailed (simplified) invoices are issued (where the invoice amount is no more than £250 inclusive of VAT) (see below)
- Credit notes issued or debit notes received for returned goods (see below)
- Sales day book and sales returns day book – to record invoices (and credit notes for returns) sent to credit customers
- Cash books – to record cash receipts
- Bank statements and paying in slips
- Records of daily takings such as till rolls
- Financial accounts

Purchases and expense records for input tax recovery

To verify **input tax**, records should include:

- Purchases and expenses invoices received – including not only standard-rated and reduced rate supplies but also those that are zero-rated and exempt
- Credit notes received or debit notes issued for returned goods (see below)
- Purchases day book and purchases returns day book – to record the invoices (and credit notes for returns) received from credit suppliers
- Cash and petty cash books – to record cash payments

A journal is needed to record non-standard transactions such as correcting errors and writing off bad debts (see later) that do not fall into any of the day books mentioned above.

Assessment focus

Note: *Have a look at the reference material to check the information about records that is provided throughout the assessment.*

A business can only reclaim input VAT if they have a valid VAT invoice. We will determine what a valid VAT invoice is below.

VAT INVOICES

Introduction

In order to reclaim input tax on a purchase, a VAT-registered trader will need to:

- Have a valid **VAT invoice**
- Use the purchased goods for business purposes.

Only VAT-registered traders can issue valid VAT invoices. These can be in either paper or electronic form.

Valid VAT invoices

If a business is registered for VAT and it makes a taxable supply to another VAT-registered business, then it must send a valid VAT invoice. If a business is registered for VAT and it makes a taxable supply to a non VAT-registered business or member of the public, a VAT invoice is not required, however one must be issued if requested.

The invoice must be issued **within 30 days of the supply.** An example is shown below:

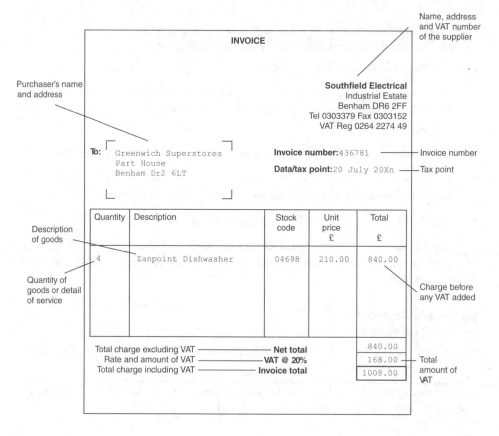

The items pointed out on the invoice above must be included on a valid VAT invoice, and are listed below:

- The supplier's name, address and registration number

- The date of issue, the tax point, if different (see later in chapter)

- A unique invoice number – this must follow on from previous invoices

- The name and address of the customer

- A description of the goods or services supplied, giving for each description the quantity, the unit price, the rate of VAT, the VAT exclusive amount, the rate of any cash or settlement discount and the total amount of VAT charged

An invoice that includes zero-rated or exempt supplies must clearly show:

- There is no VAT payable on these items, and
- The total of these values separately.

The business must keep a copy of the invoice, unless the exception for simplified (less detailed) invoices applies (see below).

If a supplier fails to issue a valid VAT invoice, there are implications for both the supplier and the customer. The supplier has failed to keep proper records, and may have filed an incorrect VAT return (for which there are penalties – see later in this text) and its customer cannot reclaim the input tax.

Assessment focus

Note: The reference material provided throughout the assessment lists what should be included on a valid VAT invoice, therefore you do not need to memorise the above list.

Effects on the VAT payable/ repayable

The issuing of a VAT invoice for standard or reduced rate supplies by a business,

- Increases the output VAT, and so
- Increases the amount payable to HMRC by the business.

The receipt of a purchase invoice for standard or reduced rate supplies by a VAT-registered business,

- Increases the input VAT, and so
- Increases the amount to be reclaimed from HMRC by the business.

Task 1

Which three of the following items must be included on a valid VAT invoice?

	✓
Customer VAT registration number	
Supplier VAT registration number	
Total VAT-exclusive amount for each type of item sold	
Total VAT amount for each type of item sold	
Total VAT-inclusive amount for each type of item sold	

Task 2

A purchase invoice for taxable supplies has just been processed. What will be the effect on VAT? Choose ONE answer.

	✓
Input tax will increase	
Input tax will decrease	
Output tax will increase	
Output tax will decrease	

Simplified (less detailed) VAT invoices

If a business is registered for VAT and it makes a taxable supply to a non VAT-registered business or member of the public, a VAT invoice is not required, however one must be issued if requested.

If the business makes a taxable supply of goods and services and the total amount is **no more than £250, including VAT**, then when a customer asks for a VAT invoice, a LESS DETAILED VAT INVOICE (sometimes referred to as a **simplified invoice**) can be issued showing:

- Seller's name, address and VAT registration number

- The time of supply (tax point)

- A description of the goods or services supplied

- For each VAT rate applicable, the total amount payable **including the VAT** and the **VAT rate** charged.

In particular, note that no details relating to the customer, or VAT-exclusive amounts are required.

Again, these details are listed on the reference material supplied in the assessment.

Exempt supplies cannot be included on a simplified invoice.

If credit cards are accepted, then a less detailed invoice can be created by adapting the sales voucher given to the customer. It must include the information listed above.

Suppliers do not need to keep copies of simplified (less detailed) invoices issued. A customer would however, need to keep a copy if they wanted to reclaim the input tax.

A VAT invoice is not required for payments of up to £25 (including VAT) for telephone calls or car park fees, or made through cash operated machines. In such cases, input tax can be claimed without a VAT invoice.

Pro forma invoice

A **pro forma invoice** is often used in order to offer goods to a potential customer at a certain price and to invite the customer to send a payment in return for which the goods will be despatched.

The potential customer cannot use the pro forma invoice as evidence to reclaim the VAT element. Therefore any pro forma invoice should be clearly marked 'THIS IS NOT A VAT INVOICE'.

If the potential customer accepts the goods or services offered to them and if the trader actually supplies them, the trader must issue a VAT invoice within the normal time limit of 30 days of supply. However, if **payment is made in advance the time limit is within 30 days of receipt of payment.**

The customer can only reclaim input tax when they receive a proper VAT invoice.

In addition to pro forma invoices, the following items are NOT VAT invoices and cannot be used to reclaim input tax:

- Invoices for only zero-rated or exempt supplies
- Invoices that state 'THIS IS NOT A VAT INVOICE'
- Statements, delivery notes or orders
- Letters, emails or other forms of correspondence.

Task 3

Decide whether the following statements are True or False. Tick the relevant boxes below.

	True ✓	False ✓
A 'simplified' invoice can be used to reclaim input VAT		
A 'pro forma' invoice can be used to reclaim input VAT		

Cash or settlement discounts

From 1 April 2015 changes to UK legislation will affect the way all businesses account for VAT when offering a prompt payment (settlement) discount. Suppliers will no longer be able to account for VAT on the discounted price but must account for VAT on the consideration actually received. However, as there are a number of valid accounting treatments for the new situation and none has so far emerged as standard practice, this change in legislation will not be reflected in this unit until September 2016 at the earliest.

CREDIT NOTES AND DEBIT NOTES

VAT-registered business receiving returned goods from a customer

If a customer returns goods then it is customary for the supplier to issue a **credit note** to reflect the value of the goods returned, including the VAT element.

Alternatively:

- The original invoice can be cancelled and recovered, and a replacement invoice issued showing the correct amount of VAT, or

- The customer may issue a debit note which reflects the value of the goods returned and the VAT element.

Credit notes and debit notes can also be issued to correct errors that have been made on the original invoice.

If a VAT-registered business issues a credit note (or receives a debit note) for returned goods, it must **record this in its accounting records** and **deduct the VAT from the amount of VAT payable** on the next VAT return.

Therefore issuing a sales credit note

- Decreases the output VAT, and so
- Decreases the amount payable to HMRC by the business.

Returning goods to a supplier

If goods are returned to a supplier then a business can obtain a **credit note**.

Alternatively:

- The business can return the original invoice to the supplier and obtain a replacement invoice showing the correct amount of VAT, or

- The business may issue a debit note to the supplier which reflects the value of the goods returned and the VAT element.

If a VAT-registered business receives a credit note (or issues a debit note) for returning goods to the supplier it must **record this in its accounting records** and **deduct the VAT from the amount of VAT reclaimable** on the next VAT return.

The receipt of a purchase credit note by a VAT-registered business,

- Decreases the input VAT, and so
- Decreases the amount to be reclaimed from HMRC by the business.

Task 4

A business issues a credit note to a customer. Which of the following statements is correct for the business?

	✓
Input tax will increase	
Input tax will decrease	
Output tax will increase	
Output tax will decrease	

TAX POINT

Introduction

VAT must be accounted for at the **time of supply.** This is known as **the 'tax point'** and determines:

- The rate of VAT to be applied to a supply. This is important where there is a change in VAT rate.

- The VAT return/**tax period** (usually quarterly) for which the output tax must be paid over to HMRC by the supplier, and the input tax can be reclaimed by the purchaser.

- The eligibility for special VAT schemes (see later in Chapter 5).

Determining the basic tax point

When goods are supplied, **the basic tax point** is the date of physical supply:

- The date on which the goods are taken away by the customer
- The date on which the goods sent to the customer, or
- The date on which the goods are made available to the customer.

When services are provided, the basic tax point is the date on which the service is carried out and all work is finished.

Exceptions to the basic tax point

The basic tax point is over-ridden if there is an **actual tax point:**

1   Firstly, an actual tax point is created if:

- The invoice is issued before the basic tax point, or
- Payment is received before the basic tax point.

Then the date of invoice or the payment is the actual tax point, depending upon which happens first.

2   Secondly, if the basic tax point still stands (ie the date of physical supply is earlier than both the invoice date and the payment date) this basic tax point can still be over-ridden if the **invoice is issued within 14 days of the basic tax point.** The invoice date will then become the actual tax point.

This 14-day rule may be varied provided that HMRC is contacted. For example an extension of the 14-day rule may be required if invoices are usually issued on a monthly basis.

If a VAT invoice is issued more than 14 days after the basic tax point without approval to extend the 14-day rule, the tax point reverts to the basic tax point, ie the date on which the goods or services were supplied.

HOW IT WORKS

The following decision tree should help you to identify the relevant tax point of a transaction:

First, identify the following three dates:

- BASIC TAX POINT (date of physical supply).
- Invoice date
- Payment date

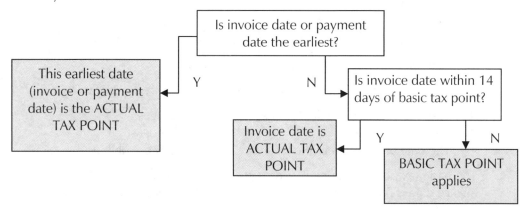

Task 5

A VAT-registered business sends goods out to a customer on 15 May 20X0. The VAT invoice is then sent later and is dated 20 May 20X0. The customer paid the invoice on 20 June 20X0. What is the tax point for these goods?

	✓
15 May 20X0	
20 May 20X0	
20 June 20X0	

As we saw earlier, sometimes suppliers send out pro forma invoices. These have no relevance for tax point. The tax point is determined based on the date of the real VAT invoice, payment or supply.

Deposits and advance payments

Sometimes customers pay a deposit in advance. If a deposit is paid, there will be separate tax points for the deposit and the balancing payment.

HOW IT WORKS

On 1 August a customer sent in a 15% deposit with an order. The goods were sent out to the customer on 6 August, and an invoice issued on 25 August. The customer paid the remaining 85% on 30 September.

The tax point for the deposit is determined by looking at:

- The basic tax point (delivery date)   6 August
- The invoice date   25 August
- The deposit payment date   1 August

Actual tax point is created as deposit is paid before the basic tax point.

Tax point for the deposit is 1 August (actual tax point)

The tax point for payment of the balance is determined by looking at:

- The basic tax point (delivery date)   6 August
- The invoice date   25 August
- The date of payment of the balance   30 September

The basic tax point is the earliest date so no actual tax point is created. Also the invoice date is more than 14 days after the basic tax point, so invoice date can be ignored.

Tax point for the balance is 6 August (basic tax point)

Task 6

A VAT-registered business received an order with a 10% deposit from a customer on 2 June 20X0. The goods were sent out to the customer on 11 June 20X0. The VAT invoice for the full amount is dated 29 June 20X0. The customer paid the remaining 90% on 31 July 20X0. Identify ONE or TWO tax point(s) for these goods.

	✓
2 June 20X0	
11 June 20X0	
29 June 20X0	
31 July 20X0	

BAD DEBT RELIEF

Introduction

As we saw above, traders usually account for VAT when they make a supply, rather than when they receive the cash for it (unless they use the cash accounting scheme – see Chapter 5).

However, just because an invoice has been issued, it does not mean that it will be paid. If the customer does not subsequently pay for the supply but the trader has accounted for the output VAT he can claim **'bad debt relief'**.

Conditions

Bad debt relief means that it is possible to reclaim the VAT that will have been paid to HMRC on that supply, provided that certain conditions are met, most importantly that:

- The debt must be more than six months overdue (note this is measured from the date when the payment was due), and less than four years and six months old.

- The debt must be written-off in the business's accounts.

- The VAT (output tax) must have been paid to HMRC, and the business did not charge more than the normal selling price for the goods.

- The debt must still belong to the business.

Making the claim

The VAT on the irrecoverable or bad debt is shown as an **increase in the input tax** to be reclaimed, NOT as a deduction from output tax.

The amount of VAT being reclaimed will be shown as a debit entry in the VAT account (increase in input tax) and included in box 4 of the VAT return. This will be covered in the next chapter.

HOW IT WORKS

An irrecoverable or bad debt arises, for example, when a customer has not paid after a long period of time or when a customer goes into liquidation.

A journal entry is made to ensure that the irrecoverable or bad debt is reflected in the accounting records. We will look at the VAT account later in the Text.

	Debit	Credit
	£	£
Bad debts expense account (net amount)	192.00	
VAT account (INPUT VAT)	38.40	
Sales ledger control account (gross amount)		230.40

Task 7

What effect will claiming VAT bad debt relief have on the amount of VAT due to HMRC? Choose ONE answer.

	✓
The amount payable will increase	
The amount payable will decrease	

Assessment focus

Don't forget, much of the information covered in this chapter is available to view throughout the live assessment within the detailed reference material. Turn to the back of the text and try to identify the areas covered within this chapter.

They include:

- *Keeping business records and VAT records*
- *Tax points*
- *VAT invoices*
- *Returned goods, credit notes, debit notes and VAT*
- *Bad debts*

The information included in this chapter will typically be tested in the following tasks:

*Task 1 Finding out about VAT, registration, **VAT records***

*Task 2 **VAT invoices, tax point**, making exempt supplies*

*Task 3 VAT schemes, due dates, **bad debt relief***

*Task 5 **VAT calculations** and reconciliations*

Performance feedback

The assessor's recent comments relevant to this chapter can be summarised as follows:

Regarding the documentation which is required by businesses, both for supply and purchase, the assessor commented:

An average performance in this task, with a number of good responses marred by a distinct lack of knowledge regarding documentation and tax points. Many students were confused by requirement to issue invoices within a specific time of the date of supply of the service and the types of documents which are acceptable.

This was particularly poor when it comes to till receipts and less detailed invoices.

The assessor also commented:

We found a general problem with accounting for VAT when deposits are taken in advance of supply or advance payments are made.

Many students failed to identify the correct VAT quarter for various scenarios.

The assessor's comments regarding the importance of accurate VAT calculations:

One of the key issues is reading the question thoroughly in order to be clear exactly what is being requested. It is difficult to do anything other than conclude that in many cases students are not diligent enough in reading questions properly, missing comments like "including VAT", or reference to the VAT to be accounted for when a deposit is required on a total invoice of a certain amount.

CHAPTER OVERVIEW

- All VAT-registered persons must keep full records of the details of all trade both within the EU and outside the EU and details of all standard-rated, reduced rate, zero-rated and exempt goods and services both purchased and sold.

- These records should normally be kept for six years and must be made available to an HMRC officer if required.

- Copies of sales invoices must be kept and the main accounting records for sales will be the sales day book, sales returns day book and the cash book.

- All invoices for purchases and expenses must be kept otherwise the input VAT cannot be reclaimed – the main accounting records for purchases and expenses are the purchases day book, the purchases returns day book and the cash book.

- A VAT-registered business making a supply to another VAT-registered business must issue a valid VAT invoice within 30 days of making the supply.

- If goods are supplied for no more than £250, including VAT, a simplified (less detailed) VAT invoice can be issued which shows only the VAT inclusive amount and the rate of VAT – however if the customer asks for a full VAT invoice, this must be supplied.

- If a pro forma invoice is sent out to a potential customer this must be clearly marked 'This is not a VAT invoice' as the customer cannot use it to reclaim any input VAT.

- The basic tax point is the date of physical supply. This basic tax point can be over-ridden by the actual tax point. The actual tax point can be created if an invoice is issued or a payment received before the goods or services are sent out, or by sending out an invoice after the supply of the goods providing that this is within 14 days of the supply.

- If a business writes-off a bad debt that is more than six months overdue and the output VAT on the supply has already been paid to HMRC, this VAT can be reclaimed from HMRC as input tax.

Keywords

Sales day book – a record of all invoices sent to credit customers

Sales returns day book – a record of all credit notes sent to credit customers

Purchases day book – a record of all invoices received from credit suppliers

Purchases returns day book – a record of all credit notes received from credit suppliers

Cash book – a record of all payments and receipts of the business

VAT invoice – a document that allows input VAT to be claimed or output VAT to be charged

Simplified (less detailed) invoice – an invoice that can be issued if the VAT-inclusive value of goods supplied is no more than £250

Pro forma invoice – often used to offer goods to potential customers. It is not a valid VAT invoice

Tax point – the date which determines when the VAT must be accounted for to HMRC

Basic tax point – the date on which goods are delivered or services provided

Actual tax point – a further date that can over-ride the basic tax point if certain conditions are met

Bad debt relief – a reclaim of output VAT when a written-off debt is more than six months overdue

TEST YOUR LEARNING

Test 1

How long does HMRC usually require relevant documents to be kept? Tick the relevant box below.

	✓
1 year	
2 years	
6 years	
20 years	

Test 2

Which TWO of the following statements about pro forma invoices are correct? Tick the relevant boxes below.

	✓
A pro forma invoice is always sent out when goods are sent to customers, before issuing the proper invoice	
A pro forma invoice should always include the words 'This is not a VAT invoice'	
A customer can reclaim VAT stated on a pro forma invoice	
A pro forma invoice is sent out to offer a customer the chance to purchase the goods detailed	

Test 3

In each of the following situations state the tax point and whether this is a basic tax point or an actual tax point (B or A):

	Date	Basic/ Actual
An invoice is sent out to a customer for goods on 22 June 20X0 and the goods are despatched on 29 June 20X0		
Goods are sent out to a customer on 18 June 20X0 and this is followed by an invoice on 23 June 20X0		
A customer pays in full for goods on 27 June 20X0 and they are then delivered to the customer on 2 July 20X0.		

Test 4

State the conditions for the VAT on an irrecoverable (bad) debt to be reclaimed from HMRC.

chapter 4:
THE VAT RETURN

chapter coverage 📖

So far we have considered the detailed rules for determining the correct amount of VAT. In this chapter we look at how this is reported to HMRC on the VAT return. The topics covered are:

✍ The VAT account

✍ The VAT return

✍ Submitting the VAT return

THE VAT ACCOUNT

Introduction

We saw in the last chapter that VAT-registered traders must keep certain records in order to correctly account for VAT. Included amongst the list of records is the **VAT account,** or as it is sometimes referred to in a business's ledger, **the VAT control account.** This is a separate record of the VAT charged on sales and the VAT paid on purchases. It provides the link between business records and the VAT return.

The trader must add up the VAT in his sales and purchases records and then transfer these totals to the VAT account, using separate headings for **VAT payable (output tax)** and **VAT deductible (input tax).**

It should also show any **adjustments for errors** discovered (see Chapter 6) or other changes, such as **bad debt relief** claims.

A VAT account can be kept in any way that suits the business, provided it contains the information described below.

The trader then uses the information from the VAT account when completing the VAT return at the end of each **VAT period** (or **tax period**) (usually every three months). We look at this later in this chapter.

VAT payable – output tax

To show the link between the output tax in the business records and the output tax on the return, the trader must have a record of:

- The output tax owed on sales.

- The output tax owed on acquisitions from other EU member states.

- Any output tax that needs to be paid following a correction or error adjustment (see Chapter 6).

Typical **entries for output tax in the VAT account** are taken from these records as follows. When added together these entries give the output tax figure to enter onto the tax return (see later in this chapter).

VAT on credit sales is taken from the VAT column of the sales day book. **VAT on cash sales** is taken from the VAT column of the cash book.

The deduction for VAT on credit notes issued to customers is taken from the VAT column of the sales returns day book.

The fuel scale charge (as we saw in Chapter 2) is a payment corresponding to the element of private fuel consumption where input VAT has been reclaimed on all fuel purchased by a business. It is shown as OUTPUT VAT on the VAT return/VAT account.

Error adjustments (in respect of output VAT) relate to non-deliberate understatement or overstatement of output tax on a previous return (see Chapter 6).

VAT deductible – input tax

To show the link between the input tax in the business records and the input tax on the return the trader must have a record of:

- The input tax the trader is able to reclaim from business purchases

- The input tax allowable on acquisitions from other EU member states

- Any input tax the trader is entitled to following a correction or error adjustment, and

- Any other necessary adjustment – such as bad debt relief.

Typical **entries for input tax in the VAT account** are taken from these records as follows. When added together these entries give the input VAT figure to enter onto the VAT return (see later in this chapter).

VAT on credit purchases is taken from the VAT column of the purchases day book.

VAT on cash purchases is taken from the VAT columns of the cash book and petty cash book.

The deduction for VAT on credit notes received from suppliers is taken from the VAT column of the purchases returns day book.

Bad debt relief is a claim for repayment of VAT already paid to HMRC on a sale to a customer who has never paid. It is shown as INPUT VAT on the VAT return/VAT account.

Error adjustments (in respect of input tax) relate to non-deliberate understatement or overstatement of input tax on a previous return (see Chapter 6).

Extract from a VAT account

Date 20XX	Reference	Debit £	Date 20XX	Reference	Credit £
1.1-31.3	Sales returns day book	X	1.1-31.3	Sales day book	X
1.1-31.3	Purchases day book	X	1.1-31.3	Cash book – UK sales	X
1.1-31.3	Cash book – UK purchases	X	1.1-31.3	Purchases returns day book – UK purchases	X
31.3	Bad debt relief	X	31.3	Fuel scale charge	X
31.3	EU acquisition reclaim	X	31.3	EU acquisition charge	X

This VAT account is presented in a traditional double entry format, meaning, for example, reductions to output such as sales returns, are shown on the debit side. *This is the preferred style of the assessor.*

Note: The VAT on **acquisitions** from other European Union countries is shown **as both output tax and input tax** as the VAT must be paid on the acquisition but can also be deducted as allowable input tax.

Tax payable

The total tax deductible (input tax) is taken away from the total tax payable (output tax) to give a **balance on the VAT account**.

If there is an excess of output VAT, this balance is the tax payable to HMRC for the period.

If the total tax payable is less than the total tax deductible, there is an excess of input VAT, and this balance is the tax reclaimable/recoverable from HMRC for the period.

VAT period

A **VAT period** (or **tax period**) is the period of time for which a business records its VAT transactions in the VAT account in order to complete the VAT return.

The VAT period usually runs for three months, with the business being allocated VAT periods when they register. A business can apply to have a tax periods that fit in with its accounting year.

One exception to quarterly three month VAT periods is if the trader uses the annual accounting scheme, where the VAT period will be 12 months long. We will see this in Chapter 5.

The trader uses the information from the VAT account when completing the VAT return at the end of each **VAT period**, and **the balance on the VAT account should agree to the figure on the VAT return.**

Clearing the VAT account

When the amount of tax due to HMRC is paid, the double entry will be to **credit the bank account** and **debit the VAT account** (or vice versa if tax is reclaimable for the period), thereby clearing the account of any balance before the postings for the next period are made.

HOW IT WORKS

In the following example a trader has output tax due to HMRC from quarter one of £2,500. The trader pays this to clear the account before the entries for quarter two are added.

Total output tax on sales for quarter two is £3,550 and total input tax on purchases is £1,750, resulting in a balance due to HMRC of £1,800.

These total amounts will be shown on the VAT return for quarter two with the balance of £1,800 being shown as VAT payable.

VAT ACCOUNT

Date 20XX	Reference	Debit £	Date 20XX	Reference	Credit £
QTR 1	VAT paid	2,500.00	QTR 1	VAT payable	2,500.00
QTR 2	Input tax on purchases	1,750.00	QTR 2	Output tax on sales	3,550.00
	Balance	1,800.00			
	Total	**6,050.00**		**Total**	**6,050.00**
			QTR 2	VAT payable	1,800.00

Assessment focus

The assessor has stated that tasks will not require you to construct a whole VAT account from scratch, but you do need to identify what sort of entries will be required.

You need to be able to reconcile a VAT return to the VAT account if an error has been made when posting to the VAT account or the VAT return. For example, a VAT payment may have been posted to the wrong side of the VAT account or not posted at all. Alternatively, a mistake may have been made when entering numbers on the VAT return meaning the balance on the VAT account does not match the amount owing to HMRC on the return. You may be asked to identify the correct explanation for the difference between the VAT account and the VAT return, or determine the balance on the VAT account after a mistake has been made.

Task 1

A trader has VAT payable to HMRC for quarter ended 31.03.20X0 of £3,750 and VAT payable for quarter ended 30.06.20X0 of £4,200. These are the correct amounts shown on the VAT returns.

The trader pays the VAT for quarter ended 31.03.20X0, but enters it onto the wrong side of the VAT account.

Identify the balance showing on the VAT account before this error is adjusted.

	✓
£7,950	
£11,700	

THE VAT RETURN

A trader must complete a VAT return for each **VAT period**.

Assessment focus

The VAT return is an extremely important area of the syllabus.

In the assessment, one task will require the preparation of specific figures for the VAT return, and another long task will concern the accurate completion of the whole VAT return. These tasks account for just over one third of the marks in the assessment.

Completing the VAT return

You will see below in section 3 that nearly all VAT-registered businesses must **submit their VAT returns online, and pay electronically.**

Assessment focus

When a return is completed online you will find some of the boxes are filled in automatically. For example, box 3 is the total of box 1 and 2 and will be totalled automatically.

This will not be the case in the assessment, all boxes will most likely need to be completed by you manually.

Below is a copy of the format of the VAT return that you can expect to see in the computer-based assessment.

VAT return for quarter ended........		£
VAT due in this period on **sales** and other outputs	Box 1	
VAT due in this period on **acquisitions** from other **EC Member States**	Box 2	
Total VAT due **(the sum of boxes 1 and 2)**	Box 3	
VAT reclaimed in this period on **purchases** and other inputs, including acquisitions from the EC	Box 4	
Net VAT to be paid to HM Revenue & Customs or reclaimed by you **(Difference between boxes 3 and 4 - if Box 4 is greater than Box 3, use a minus sign)**	Box 5	
Total value of **sales** and all other outputs excluding any VAT. **Include your box 8 figure. Whole pounds only**	Box 6	
Total value of **purchases** and all other inputs excluding any VAT. **Include your box 9 figure. Whole pounds only**	Box 7	
Total value of all **supplies** of goods and related costs, excluding any VAT, to other **EC Member States. Whole pounds only**	Box 8	
Total value of all **acquisitions** of goods and related costs, excluding any VAT, from other **EC Member States. Whole pounds only**	Box 9	

Information for boxes 1 – 4 can usually be extracted from the VAT account.

The boxes are completed as follows:

Box 1 **VAT due in this period on sales and other outputs:**

- The total of the output VAT on sales (include credit and cash sales)

- Less the VAT on any credit notes issued

- Plus any fuel scale charges

- Plus adjustments for earlier period errors (see Chapter 6).

Box 2 The **VAT due on any acquisitions** from other EU countries.

Box 3 The total of boxes 1 and 2.

Box 4 **VAT reclaimed in this period on purchases and other inputs, including acquisitions from the EC:**

- The total of the input VAT on purchases and expenses (include credit and cash purchases)

- Less the VAT on any credit notes received

57

- Plus the VAT on any acquisitions from other EU countries
- Plus bad debt relief
- Plus adjustments for earlier period errors (see Chapter 6).

Box 5 **Net VAT to be paid to HM Revenue & Customs or reclaimed by you:**

- Deduct box 4 (input tax) from box 3 (output tax)
- If box 3 (output tax) > box 4 (input tax), then tax is payable to HMRC
- If box 4 (input tax) > box 3 (output tax), then tax is reclaimable from HMRC

Boxes 6-9 deal with sales and purchases before any VAT is added. Accounting records such as purchases day books, sales day books and journals will be needed to complete these figures. Note that boxes 6-9 are stated in whole pounds (ie no pence are needed).

Box 6 **Total value of sales and all other outputs excluding any VAT:**

This is the total of all sales **less credit notes issued** excluding VAT. It includes:

- Standard-rated sales
- Zero-rated sales (including exports)
- Exempt sales
- Supplies to EU member countries (despatches)

Box 7 **Total value of purchases and all other inputs excluding any VAT:**

This is the total of all purchases and other expenses **less credit notes received** excluding VAT. It includes:

- Standard-rated supplies (including standard-rated imports)
- Zero-rated supplies (including zero-rated imports)
- Exempt supplies
- Acquisitions from EU member countries

Box 8 **Total value of all supplies of goods and related costs, excluding any VAT, to other EC Member States:**

Note: this figure is also included in box 6.

For the purposes of this assessment, you should not include in Box 8 the value of goods supplied to EU customers who are not VAT-registered.

Box 9   **Total value of all acquisitions of goods and related costs, excluding any VAT, from other EC Member States:**

Note: this figure is also included in box 7.

(Related costs includes items such as freight costs and insurance for the goods.)

The **value** of the supply or acquisition of goods from other EU countries is shown on the VAT return separately. This is used to provide information on movements of taxable goods within the EU.

HOW IT WORKS

This example shows how the business and accounting records are likely to be presented to you in the assessment.

The relevant ledger accounts are shown below for quarter ended 31.3.20XX.

Sales and sales returns account

Date 20XX	Reference	Debit £	Date 20XX	Reference	Credit £
1.1-31.3	Sales returns day book – UK sales	2,374.00	1.1-31.3	Sales day book – UK sales	52,111.00
			1.1-31.3	Sales day book – EU despatches	9,700.00
			1.1-31.3	Sales day book – exports	4,259.00
31.3	Balance c/d	74,041.00	1.1-31.3	Cash book – UK sales	10,345.00
	Total	76,415.00		Total	76,415.00

Purchases and purchases returns account

Date 20XX	Reference	Debit £	Date 20XX	Reference	Credit £
1.1-31.3	Purchases day book – UK purchases	17,980.00	1.1-31.3	Purchases returns day book – UK purchases	1,020.00
1.1-31.3	Purchases day book – EU acquisitions	3,256.00			
1.1-31.3	Purchases day book – zero-rated imports	2,220.00	31.3	Balance c/d	22,436.00
	Total	23,456.00		Total	23,456.00

VAT account

Date 20XX	Reference	Debit £	Date 20XX	Reference	Credit £
1.1-31.3	Sales returns day book	474.80	1.1-31.3	Sales day book	10,422.20
1.1-31.3	Purchases day book	3,596.00	1.1-31.3	Cash book – UK sales	2,069.00
			1.1-31.3	Purchases returns day book – UK purchases	204.00

The following journal entry has been made to reflect a bad debt that is to be recoverable this quarter.

	Debit £	Credit £
Bad debts expense account (net amount)	975.00	
VAT account	195.00	
Sales ledger control account (gross amount)		1,170.00

In addition, you are told that a fuel scale charge of £28.83 applies for the private use for an employee's car and VAT on EU acquisitions is £651.20.

EU despatches are to VAT-registered customers.

How to complete the VAT return

Now to complete the boxes. Note that figures are shown in pounds and pence in boxes 1-5, with the figures being rounded down (if necessary) to pounds for boxes 6-9.

Workings:

		£
Box 1	VAT on sales from the sales day book	10,422.20
	VAT on sales from the cash book	2,069.00
	Fuel scale charge	28.83
	Less: VAT on credit notes	(474.80)
		12,045.23
Box 2	VAT due on EU acquisitions	651.20
Box 3	Total of box 1 and box 2 £12,045.23 + £651.20	12,696.43
Box 4	VAT on purchases from purchases day book	3,596.00
	VAT on EU acquisitions	651.20
	Bad debt relief	195.00
	Less: VAT on credit notes from suppliers	(204.00)
		4,238.20
Box 5	Net VAT due Box 3 minus box 4	
	£12,696.43 − £4,238.20	8,458.23
Box 6	Standard-rated credit UK sales	52,111.00
	Less: standard-rated credit notes	(2,374.00)
	Cash sales	10,345.00
	EU despatches	9,700.00
	Exports	4,259.00
		74,041
Box 7	Standard-rated credit purchases	17,980.00
	Less: standard-rated credit notes	(1,020.00)
	EU acquisitions	3,256.00
	Imports	2,220.00
		22,436
Box 8	EU sales	9,700
Box 9	EU acquisitions	3,256

VAT return for quarter ended 31.3.20XX		£
VAT due in this period on **sales** and other outputs	Box 1	12,045.23
VAT due in this period on **acquisitions** from other **EC Member States**	Box 2	651.20
Total VAT due (**the sum of boxes 1 and 2**)	Box 3	12,696.43
VAT reclaimed in this period on **purchases** and other inputs, including acquisitions from the EC	Box 4	4,238.20
Net VAT to be paid to HM Revenue & Customs or reclaimed by you (**Difference between boxes 3 and 4 - if Box 4 is greater than Box 3, use a minus sign**)	Box 5	8,458.23
Total value of **sales** and all other outputs excluding any VAT. **Include your box 8 figure. Whole pounds only**	Box 6	74,041
Total value of **purchases** and all other inputs excluding any VAT. **Include your box 9 figure. Whole pounds only**	Box 7	22,436
Total value of all **supplies** of goods and related costs, excluding any VAT, to other **EC Member States. Whole pounds only**	Box 8	9,700
Total value of all **acquisitions** of goods and related costs, excluding any VAT, from other **EC Member States. Whole pounds only**	Box 9	3,256

Complete the VAT account

Once the journal entries are completed for bad debt relief, the fuel scale charge and the EU acquisition, the VAT account should agree to the VAT payable on the return.

BPP
LEARNING MEDIA

VAT account

Date 20XX	Reference	Debit £	Date 20XX	Reference	Credit £
1.1-31.3	Sales returns day book	474.80	1.1-31.3	Sales day book	10,422.20
1.1-31.3	Purchases day book	3,596.00	1.1-31.3	Cash book – UK sales	2,069.00
31.3	Bad debt relief	195.00	1.1-31.3	Purchases returns day book – UK purchases	204.00
31.3	EU acquisition reclaim	651.20	31.3	Fuel scale charge	28.83
31.3	BALANCE b/d	8,458.23	31.3	EU acquisition charge	651.20
	Total	13,375.23		Total	13,375.23
				VAT payable	8,458.23

Assessment focus

The example above shows how the business and accounting records are likely to be presented to you in the assessment, showing relevant quarterly ledger accounts.

You will be expected to extract figures from the general ledger accounts, eg sales and sales returns accounts, purchases and purchases returns accounts etc. to complete the VAT return. However, you will also need to know that the figures in each of these accounts come from books of prime or original entry.

Task 2

Identify which ONE of the following statements in relation to acquisition of goods from other EU countries and how they are dealt with on the VAT return is correct.

	✓
Input tax paid at the ports is reclaimed as input tax on the VAT return	
Both input tax and output tax in relation to the goods are shown on the VAT return	
They are zero-rated and so no VAT features on the VAT return	
They are exempt and so no VAT features on the VAT return	

Task 3

Identify which of the following statement(s) is/are correct. There may be more than one correct statement.

	✓
The fuel scale charge increases output VAT and is shown in Box 1	
VAT on EU acquisitions increases both input VAT and output VAT and is shown in boxes 1 & 4	
Credit notes received from suppliers reduce input VAT and are shown in box 4	
Credit notes issued to customers reduce output VAT and are shown in box 1	

Task 4

Vincent is VAT-registered and sells standard-rated items both in the UK and overseas. Sales (excluding VAT) for the quarter ended 31.3.X0 are split as follows:

- UK sales – £27,200.00
- Exports (outside EU) – £9,705.00
- Despatches (within EU) to VAT-registered customers – £18,345.00
- Despatches (within EU) to non VAT-registered customers – £7,200.00

Complete the following extract of the VAT return

VAT return for quarter ended 31.03.20X0		£
VAT due in this period on **sales** and other outputs	Box 1	
Total value of **sales** and all other outputs excluding any VAT. **Include your box 8 figure. Whole pounds only**	Box 6	
Total value of all **supplies** of goods and related costs, excluding any VAT, to other **EC Member States. Whole pounds only**	Box 8	

Task 5

Valerie is VAT-registered and purchases standard-rated items for her business both in the UK and overseas. Purchases (excluding VAT) for the quarter ended 31.3.X0 are split as follows:

- UK purchases – £9,230.00
- Imports (outside EU) – £1,205.00
- Acquisitions (within EU) from VAT-registered suppliers – £8,345.00

Complete the following extract of the VAT return

VAT return for quarter ended 31.03.20X0		£
VAT due in this period on **acquisitions** from other **EC Member States**	Box 2	
VAT reclaimed in the period on **purchases** and other inputs, including acquisitions from the EC	Box 4	
Total value of purchases and all other inputs excluding any VAT. **Include your box 9 figure. Whole pounds only**	Box 7	
Total value of all **acquisitions** of goods and related costs, excluding any VAT, from other **EC Member States. Whole pounds only**	Box 9	

SUBMITTING THE VAT RETURN

Almost all VAT-registered traders must submit their VAT returns online and pay VAT electronically.

The return

Previously, the **normal due date** for submitting the VAT return was **one calendar month after the end of the relevant VAT return period.**

However, when a VAT return is submitted online (which is now mandatory for almost all VAT registered traders) the VAT return is due **one month and seven calendar days after the end of the relevant VAT return period.**

For example if a business prepares a VAT return for the period to 31 December 2015, it must submit the return by 7 February 2016.

However, traders using the annual accounting scheme have a different due date (see Chapter 5). Also 'substantial' traders, who make VAT payments on account throughout the VAT period, must always submit their returns one calendar month after the end of the VAT return period.

The due dates for submitting the return and making payment can be found on the return.

Payment deadlines

The VAT payable, as shown on the return (box 5), is due for payment by the same date as the return must be submitted. The trader is responsible for ensuring the payment clears in HMRC's bank account on time.

The exception to this is if payment is made by online direct debit, in which case HMRC will collect payment three working days after the one month and seven days deadline.

If a trader does not have cleared funds in HMRC's website by the payment deadline he may be liable for a **late payment surcharge** (as described in Chapter 6).

Repayment of VAT

If the total of box 4 (VAT reclaimable) is greater than the total in box 3 (VAT payable) the figure in box 5 will be negative and a repayment will be due from HMRC.

HMRC are obliged to automatically schedule the repayment, provided certain checks have been carried out to make sure the repayment is in fact due, and there are, for example, no outstanding debts owed by the business.

Assessment focus

Don't forget, much of the information covered in this chapter is available to view throughout the live assessment within the detailed reference material, including a section on completing the VAT return, box by box.

Turn to the back of the text and try to identify the areas covered within this chapter.

They include:

- *Keeping a VAT account*
- *Completing the VAT return box by box*
- *VAT periods, submitting returns and paying VAT*

In particular, make sure you read all the paragraphs about filing and payment due dates carefully, so you remember to add the seven extra calendar days for online filing and electronic payment (relevant to almost all businesses).

The information included in this chapter will typically be tested in the following tasks:

Task 3 VAT schemes, **due dates,** bad debt relief

Task 5 VAT calculations and **reconciliations**

Task 6 **Preparing specific figures for the VAT return**

Task 7 **Completing and submitting a VAT return accurately**

Task 8 **Communicating VAT information**

We look at how the VAT return submission and payment dates may feature in a communication task (task 8) in more detail in Chapter 6.

Performance feedback

The assessor's recent comments relevant to this chapter can be summarised as follows:

Students may need to be able to reconcile the values on the VAT return to a formal VAT account in the general ledger (task 5).

It is clear that students find this type of task challenging with just less than half attaining the required competence when this was recently tested. The accounting and reconciliation side was where the common problems were.

Students need to understand that working out VAT is only part of the issue for businesses; it is also a statutory requirement to account for the VAT correctly and to ensure the VAT account matches the return submitted to HMRC. The authorities will check the VAT account to ensure this is correct.

It is important to note how the assessment is designed to test and elicit knowledge of how VAT is constructed. Questions seek to establish if students can identify what sort of entries will be required rather than attempting to construct a VAT account from scratch. Once again close reading of the task and the options is needed to match the correct option to the question.

Regarding the task on preparing specific figures for the VAT return (task 6), the assessor has the following comments:

This task covers the issue of making the necessary calculations ready for the formal VAT return to be submitted by the business. Students have to be able to assess the information provided for them and derive from this the different values needed for entering onto the return.

In particular students need to be able to deal with [sales/purchase] returns, both to and from the business, as well as discounts, bad debts and the different types of supply.

A common problem is when students do not appear to read the whole question, perhaps not taking enough time to assimilate all the information provided to them. This is somewhat understandable given the amount of information, however success in this type of task can only come from spending just that little bit extra time to make sure all the information has been absorbed.

Generally students appear to fail to allow for [sales/purchases] returns in the computation, or alternatively they use the returns value but in the wrong manner.

Another problem for many students is allocating the bad debt relief to the correct part of the account and then working out the appropriate sum to enter into the return. Relief for bad debts is given by HM Revenue & Customs in a specific manner and the instructions are very clear –

> *"If you are entitled to claim Bad Debt Relief, you add the amount of VAT you are reclaiming on your purchases (input tax) and put the total figure in Box 4 of your VAT Return." HMRC*

Too many students adjust the Box 1 figure or ignore the bad debt relief when they enter their figures.

Finally, inevitable in a complex computational task, there are often a number of arithmetical errors.

Regarding the task on completing and submitting a VAT return accurately (task 7), the assessor has the following comments:

This is one of the most important tasks in the assessment, that being where the students show how to complete the final, formal, return to be submitted to HM Revenue & Customs. The assessment uses images similar to the ones students would meet in real life and attempts to mirror the online return format.

Students have to demonstrate their ability to complete this return form correctly and within the deadlines laid down by HMRC. Businesses face significant penalties for failure to comply and hence employers expect qualified staff to be able to do this work unsupervised.

Encouragingly we find this to be the task with the best performance across students with very few failing to achieve competence and well over half exceeding the competence required.

The assessment may also require VAT return and payment deadlines to be communicated internally within a business. However, the assessor's most recent comments regarding the communication task are given in Chapter 6 when communication is discussed in greater detail.

CHAPTER OVERVIEW

- The VAT account records the VAT payable and deductible by the business and is a link between the business records and the VAT return.

- Normally every quarter the VAT return must be completed and submitted to HMRC together with any payment by the due date.

- The first five boxes of the VAT return can usually be completed from the figures in the VAT account.

- Boxes 6 to 9 must be completed from the other accounting records of the business showing sales and purchases, despatches and acquisitions excluding VAT.

- The VAT return is generally due one month and seven days following the end of the relevant VAT return period.

Keywords

VAT account – the ledger account in which all amounts of input tax and output tax are recorded

VAT return – the form which must be completed to show the amount of VAT due or to be reclaimed, usually for the quarter

TEST YOUR LEARNING

Test 1

Decide whether the following statements are True or False. Tick the relevant boxes below.

	True ✓	False ✓
If input VAT is greater than output VAT on the return, VAT is payable to HMRC		
If output VAT is greater than input VAT on the return, VAT is repayable from HMRC		

Test 2

Holly completed her VAT return for the latest quarter. It correctly indicates that she owes HMRC £7,520 VAT. However her VAT account is showing an amount due of £12,220. VAT payable for the previous quarter was £4,700.

Tick which ONE of the following statements explains the difference:

	✓
The payment of £4,700 for the previous quarter has been included twice in the VAT account	
The payment of £4,700 for the previous quarter has been omitted from the VAT account	

Test 3

The ledger accounts of a VAT-registered trader for quarter ended 30.6.20XX are shown below:

Sales and sales returns account

Date 20XX	Reference	Debit £	Date 20XX	Reference	Credit £
1.4-30.6	Sales returns day book – UK sales	2,400.00	1.4-30.6	Sales day book – UK sales	26,000.00
			1.4-30.6	Sales day book – exports	5,800.00
30.6	Balance c/d	43,400.00	1.4-30.6	Cash book – UK sales	14,000.00
	Total	**45,800.00**		**Total**	**45,800.00**

Purchases account

Date 20XX	Reference	Debit £	Date 20XX	Reference	Credit £
1.4-30.6	Purchases day book – UK purchases	15,500.00			
1.4-30.6	Purchases day book – EU acquisitions	3,750.00	30.6	Balance c/d	19,250.00
	Total	**19,250.00**		**Total**	**19,250.00**

VAT account

Date 20XX	Reference	Debit £	Date 20XX	Reference	Credit £
1.4-30.6	Sales returns day book	480.00	1.4-30.6	Sales day book	5,200.00
1.4-30.6	Purchases day book	3,100.00	1.4-30.6	Cash book – UK sales	2,800.00

In addition, you are told that bad debt relief on a sales invoice of £500.00 excluding VAT is to be claimed this quarter.

VAT on EU acquisitions is £750.00.

Complete boxes 1 to 9 of the VAT return below for quarter ended 30.6.20XX.

VAT return for quarter ended 30.6.20XX		£
VAT due in this period on **sales** and other outputs	Box 1	
VAT due in this period on **acquisitions** from other **EC Member States**	Box 2	
Total VAT due (**the sum of boxes 1 and 2**)	Box 3	
VAT reclaimed in this period on **purchases** and other inputs, including acquisitions from the EC	Box 4	
Net VAT to be paid to HM Revenue & Customs or reclaimed by you (**Difference between boxes 3 and 4 - if Box 4 is greater than Box 3, use a minus sign**)	Box 5	
Total value of **sales** and all other outputs excluding any VAT. **Include your box 8 figure. Whole pounds only**	Box 6	
Total value of **purchases** and all other inputs excluding any VAT. **Include your box 9 figure. Whole pounds only**	Box 7	
Total value of all **supplies** of goods and related costs, excluding any VAT, to other **EC Member States. Whole pounds only**	Box 8	
Total value of all **acquisitions** of goods and related costs, excluding any VAT, from other **EC Member States. Whole pounds only**	Box 9	

Test 4

The following ledger accounts are shown below of a VAT-registered trader for quarter ended 31 May 20XX.

Sales and sales returns account

Date 20XX	Reference	Debit £	Date 20XX	Reference	Credit £
1.3-31.5	Sales returns day book – UK standard-rated sales	398.86	1.3-31.5	Sales day book – UK standard-rated sales	30,678.25
1.3-31.5	Sales returns day book – UK zero-rated sales	25.59	1.3-31.5	Sales day book – UK zero-rated sales	3,581.67
31.5	Balance c/d	38,890.28	1.3-31.5	Cash book - UK standard-rated sales	5,054.51
	Total	39,314.43		Total	39,314.43

Purchases account

Date 20XX	Reference	Debit £	Date 20XX	Reference	Credit £
1.3-31.5	Purchases day book – UK standard-rated purchases	20,450.85			
1.3-31.5	Purchases day book – UK zero-rated purchases	2,669.80			
1.3-31.5	Cash book – UK standard-rated purchases/ expenses	3,033.01	31.5	Balance c/d	26,153.66
	Total	26,153.66		Total	26,153.66

VAT account

Date 20XX	Reference	Debit £	Date 20XX	Reference	Credit £
1.3-31.5	Sales returns day book	79.77	1.3-31.5	Sales day book	6,135.65
1.3-31.5	Purchases day book	4,090.17	1.3-31.5	Cash book	1,010.90
1.3-31.5	Cash book	606.60			

Journal (extract)

	Debit	Credit
	£	£
Irrecoverable (bad) debts expense	192.00	
VAT account	38.40	
Receivables (debtors) (VAT inclusive at 20%)		230.40

Complete boxes 1 to 9 of the VAT return for quarter ended 31 May 20XX

VAT return for quarter ended		£
VAT due in this period on **sales** and other outputs	Box 1	
VAT due in this period on **acquisitions** from other **EC Member States**	Box 2	
Total VAT due (**the sum of boxes 1 and 2**)	Box 3	
VAT reclaimed in this period on **purchases** and other inputs, including acquisitions from the EC	Box 4	
Net VAT to be paid to HM Revenue & Customs or reclaimed by you (**Difference between boxes 3 and 4 – if Box 4 is greater than Box 3, use a minus sign**)	Box 5	
Total value of **sales** and all other outputs excluding any VAT. **Include your box 8 figure. Whole pounds only**	Box 6	
Total value of **purchases** and all other inputs excluding any VAT. **Include your box 9 figure. Whole pounds only**	Box 7	
Total value of all **supplies** of goods and related costs, excluding any VAT, to other **EC Member States. Whole pounds only**	Box 8	
Total value of all **acquisitions** of goods and related costs, excluding any VAT, from other **EC Member States. Whole pounds only**	Box 9	

chapter 5:
SCHEMES FOR SMALL BUSINESSES

─── **chapter coverage** 📖 ───

Over many years it has been recognised that VAT administration has become a burden for small businesses. Several schemes have been devised in order to help such businesses. The topics covered in this chapter are:

✍ Standard accounting

✍ Annual accounting scheme

✍ Cash accounting scheme

✍ Flat rate scheme

STANDARD ACCOUNTING

We saw in the last chapter that generally a VAT-registered trader will need to complete a **VAT return every three months** (known as a 'quarter').

Sometimes a trader may choose to complete a VAT return every month. This would be advantageous for a trader who regularly claims a repayment from HMRC. A typical example is a trader making zero-rated supplies, who would not be charging output tax to its customers, but who would still be able to reclaim input tax on purchases.

Some very large ('substantial') traders are required to make monthly payments on account for their quarterly returns.

The schemes outlined below have been introduced in order to try and ease the administrative burden of standard accounting and improve cash flow for small businesses.

ANNUAL ACCOUNTING SCHEME

Introduction

The annual accounting scheme is helpful to small businesses as it cuts down the administrative burden of VAT by allowing the business to **submit one VAT return every 12 months,** rather than each quarter.

The VAT return is due within two months of the end of the 12 month tax period.

Conditions

The limits for joining and leaving this scheme are:

	VAT-exclusive taxable turnover
VAT-registered traders can join the scheme if **turnover** (excluding capital supplies) **in the next 12 months is expected to be no more than**	£1,350,000
Traders must leave the scheme if **turnover in the previous 12 months exceeds,** or if **estimated** turnover **exceeds**	£1,600,000

The business must be up to date with all VAT returns and payments, and alongside using the annual accounting scheme, can also use either the cash accounting scheme or the flat rate scheme (but not both).

Operation

Under this scheme the business:

- Makes nine (usually) equal monthly direct debit payments of **1/10 of the VAT liability for the previous year**.

  If the business has been VAT registered for less than 12 months**, the payments will be based on an estimate of** the liability for the first year.

- The first monthly payment is due at the end of month four during the year, working through to the end of month 12.

- **The balancing payment will be due with the VAT return, within two months after the year end.** If the total of the nine monthly payments exceeds the final VAT liability, then a balancing refund is due.

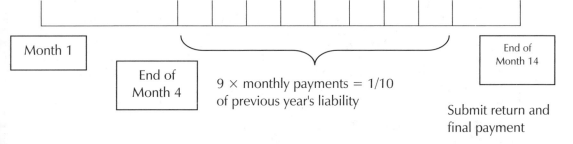

Month 1

End of Month 4

9 × monthly payments = 1/10 of previous year's liability

End of Month 14

Submit return and final payment

HOW IT WORKS

A VAT-registered trader has been allocated a VAT year end of 31 May. For the year ended 31 May 20X1 the liability was £55,000. The liability for year ended 31 May 20X2 turns out to be £62,000.

The VAT for year ended 31 May 20X2 would be paid as follows:

Month 4	30 September X1	£55,000 × 10%	£5,500
Month 5	31 October X1	£55,000 × 10%	£5,500
Month 6	30 November X1	£55,000 × 10%	£5,500
Month 7	31 December X1	£55,000 × 10%	£5,500
Month 8	31 January X2	£55,000 × 10%	£5,500
Month 9	28 February X2	£55,000 × 10%	£5,500
Month 10	31 March X2	£55,000 × 10%	£5,500
Month 11	30 April X2	£55,000 × 10%	£5,500
Month 12	31 May X2	£55,000 × 10%	£5,500
	Total instalments		£49,500
Within 2 months of year end	1 July X2	Balance £62,000-£49,500	£12,500

Advantages and disadvantages of the scheme

The advantages of the annual accounting scheme include:

- Only one VAT return each year instead of four
- Two months instead of one month and seven days to complete and send the return and payment
- Ability to manage cash flow more accurately by paying fixed amounts in each instalment
- Traders can join the scheme immediately from date of VAT registration

The disadvantages of the annual accounting scheme include:

- If turnover decreases, the interim payments may be higher than the VAT payments would be under normal VAT accounting
- Must wait until the end of the year to receive any refund
- If regularly reclaim VAT, will only get one repayment per year

Task 1

A trader has joined the annual accounting scheme for the year ended 31 December 2015. Identify whether the following statement is True or False.

	True	False
	✓	✓
The first payment due to HMRC is by 1 April 2015.		

CASH ACCOUNTING SCHEME

Introduction

The cash accounting scheme enables a business to **account for tax on the basis of cash paid and received**, rather than under the normal tax point rules. Effectively, the tax point of the supply becomes the day in which cash changes hands.

This means that a registered trader accounts for output tax when a customer actually pays for the goods or services. The trader accounts for input tax on purchases when the supplier is actually paid.

Conditions

The limits for joining and leaving this scheme are:

	VAT-exclusive taxable turnover
VAT-registered traders can join the scheme if **turnover** (excluding capital supplies) **in the next 12 months is expected to be no more than**	£1,350,000
Traders must leave the scheme if **turnover in the previous 12 months exceeds**	£1,600,000

The business:

- Must have a clean record with HMRC, and

- Must not have been convicted of a VAT offence or penalty in the previous 12 months, and

- All VAT returns and payments must be up-to-date.

If a business uses the cash accounting scheme, they may also be able to use the annual accounting scheme.

Advantages and disadvantages

The scheme provides automatic relief from irrecoverable (bad) debts since no output VAT is payable to HMRC if the customer does not pay.

The scheme is also very useful for:

- A business which gives its customers a **long period of credit or they are slow to pay,** as it will not have to pay output tax until it is received.

  Therefore OUTPUT VAT will be paid to HMRC later than if the business used the standard VAT accounting rules.

- A business that **pays its suppliers promptly**, with INPUT VAT being reclaimed at the same time or earlier than with standard rules.

The scheme would be less beneficial for:

- A business which receives a **long period of credit from its suppliers, or is slow to pay,** as they would not be able to reclaim the input tax until they have paid their suppliers.

- A business which **receives payment promptly** from its customers, as they may end up paying output tax earlier than with the standard rules.

VAT return and payment dates are as for the standard scheme, unless the business is also in the annual accounting scheme.

Assessment focus

Further disadvantages dealing with repayments when starting to trade, and leaving the scheme are listed in the reference material. It is advisable to perhaps look at these once you have got to grips with the disadvantages relating to timing principles as outlined above.

Task 2

Would the cash accounting scheme improve the cash flow of a retail business that receives most of its sales in cash and buys most of its purchases on credit? Tick ONE of the boxes.

	✓
Yes, because they would be able to reclaim input VAT earlier	
Yes, because they would pay output VAT later	
No, because they would reclaim input VAT later	
No, because they would pay output VAT earlier	

FLAT RATE SCHEME

Introduction

The flat rate scheme allows a business to simplify its VAT accounting by **calculating the VAT payment due as a flat percentage of VAT-inclusive turnover.**

Conditions

The limits for joining and leaving this scheme are:

	Turnover
VAT-registered traders can join the scheme if **VAT-exclusive TAXABLE turnover** (excluding capital supplies) does not exceed	£150,000
Traders must leave the scheme if **TOTAL value of VAT-inclusive turnover** exceeds	£230,000

Notice the difference between the turnover to be included in each limit. The limit for joining the scheme only includes **taxable** turnover, but uses the **VAT-exclusive** amount. However, the limit for leaving the scheme includes all turnover (**taxable and exempt supplies**) and uses the **VAT-inclusive** amount.

If a business uses the flat rate scheme, they may also be able to use the annual accounting scheme.

Operation

Businesses using the scheme:

- Apply a flat rate percentage to **total VAT-inclusive** turnover for the period, and this becomes the amount payable to HMRC

- Cannot reclaim (input) VAT on purchases (with exceptions)

- Need to issue normal VAT invoices to their VAT-registered customers

- Do not have to record all the details of invoices issued or purchase invoices received to calculate VAT due.

HMRC set different flat rate percentages for different trade sectors ranging from 4% to 14.5%. This percentage is applied to the **VAT-inclusive** turnover of the business, which **includes all zero rate and exempt income along with the standard rate income.**

VAT returns and payments are made at the same time as for the standard scheme, unless the business is also in the annual accounting scheme.

Advantages and disadvantages

The main advantages of this scheme are:

- It simplifies the administration considerably, as the VAT on each individual sales and purchase invoice does not have to be recorded (although VAT is still charged to customers as normal).

- There may be less VAT payable to HMRC than under the normal rules.

- Cash flow can be managed more easily as there is always a certainty as to what percentage of turnover will be paid to HMRC.

- A discount is given in the first year of VAT registration of 1% reduction to the flat rate.

The main disadvantages of this scheme are:

- Input VAT cannot (generally) be reclaimed on purchases and expenses.

- The flat rate percentage is applied to all turnover including zero-rated and exempt supplies.

This may result in more VAT payable than under standard VAT accounting rules, and so might not be suitable for the following type of businesses:

- Those in a trade with a high flat rate percentage.

- Those making a lot of zero-rated or exempt supplies.

- Those who regularly receive a VAT repayment under standard VAT accounting.

- Those whose purchases and expenses are mainly standard-rated.

Task 3

A trader, making standard-rated (20%) supplies, has joined the flat rate scheme.

The flat rate percentage applying to his business sector is 8.5%.

His VAT-exclusive turnover for the quarter is £30,000.

What is the VAT due to HMRC for the quarter?

	✓
£2,550	
£3,060	

Don't forget, much of the information covered in this chapter is available to view throughout the live assessment within the detailed reference material. Turn to the back of the text and try to identify the areas covered within this chapter.

They include:

- *Special accounting schemes:*
  - *Annual accounting scheme*
  - *Cash accounting scheme*
  - *Flat rate scheme*

You should notice that considerable detail is available to view on these three schemes.

The information included in this chapter will typically be tested in the following task:

*Task 3 **VAT schemes,** due dates, bad debt relief*

Performance feedback

The assessor's recent comments relevant to this chapter can be summarised as follows:

There appears to be a reasonable knowledge of the basics of VAT schemes but the concern here is that any calculations carried out demonstrate a lack of understanding of how it works in practice. Students also seemed to be poor in respect of the understanding of the rules for entering and leaving the various schemes and since there can be a lack of consistency in the statutory rules it is important that students know this. There is ample guidance available.

CHAPTER OVERVIEW

- If a VAT-registered business has an annual turnover of no more than £1,350,000 excluding VAT, it may be eligible for the annual accounting scheme – under which nine monthly direct debit payments are made, usually based upon the previous year's VAT liability. The tenth balancing payment is made when the VAT return for the year is submitted within two months of the year end.

- If a VAT-registered business has an annual turnover of no more than £1,350,000 excluding VAT, it may be eligible for the cash accounting scheme – under which VAT has to be accounted for to HMRC on the basis of cash payments received and made, rather than under the normal tax point rules.

- If a VAT-registered business has an annual turnover of no more than £150,000 excluding VAT, it may be eligible for the flat rate scheme – under which it can simplify its VAT records by calculating its VAT payment as a percentage of total (VAT-inclusive) turnover instead of recording the input and output tax on each individual purchase and sales invoice.

Keywords

Annual accounting scheme – a method of accounting for VAT which does not require quarterly returns and payments – instead it requires nine monthly direct debit payments and one annual return accompanied by the final balancing payment

Cash accounting scheme – a method of accounting for VAT which allows VAT to be dealt with according to the date of payment or receipt of cash rather than under the normal tax point rules

Flat rate scheme – enables businesses to calculate their VAT payment as a percentage of total VAT-inclusive turnover

TEST YOUR LEARNING

Test 1

Complete the following letter to Jacob Lymstock, a client of yours who has had a small business for several years.

AN accountant
Number Street
London
SW11 8AB

Mr Lymstock
Alphabet Street
London
W12 6WM

Dear Mr Lymstock
ANNUAL ACCOUNTING SCHEME

I have recently been reviewing your files. I would like to make you aware of a scheme that you could use for VAT.

As the annual value of your taxable supplies, [_____ ▼] (1) VAT and supplies of capital items, in the following 12 months is expected to be [_____ ▼] (2) [_____ ▼] (3) you can join the annual accounting scheme.

Under this scheme you make [_____ ▼] (4) monthly direct debit payments based on your VAT liability for the previous year. The first of these payments is due at the end of the [_____ ▼] (5) month of the accounting period. You must then prepare a VAT return for the year and submit it with the balancing payment, by [_____ ▼] (6) after the year end.

Use of this annual accounting scheme is a great help as it means that you only have to prepare [_____ ▼] (7) VAT return(s) each year.

If you wish to discuss this with me in more detail please do not hesitate to contact me.

Your sincerely

AN Accountant

Picklist:
(1) including / excluding
(2) no more than / greater than
(3) £1,350,000 / £1,600,000
(4) 4 / 9 / 10 / 12
(5) first / fourth / twelfth
(6) 30 days / one month / two months
(7) one / four / 12

Test 2

Complete the following statement using the picklist below.

If the annual value of taxable supplies, [▼] (1) VAT, is [▼] (2) than [▼] (3) and provided that a trader has a clean record with HMRC, he may be able to apply to use the cash accounting scheme.

The scheme allows the accounting for VAT to be based upon the date of [▼] (4). This is particularly useful for a business which gives its customers a [▼] (5) period of credit whilst paying its suppliers promptly.

The scheme also gives automatic relief [▼] (6) so if the customer does not pay the amount due, then the VAT need not be accounted for to HMRC.

Picklist:

(1) including / excluding
(2) no more / greater
(3) £1,350,000 / £1,600,000
(4) receipt and payment of money / invoice
(5) long / short
(6) from filing VAT returns / for bad debts

Test 3

An existing trader makes standard rated supplies and uses the flat rate scheme. The flat rate percentage that he must use is 11.5%.

For quarter ended 31 Mar 20X0 the trader had total turnover of £9,500 excluding VAT. He also had VAT-exclusive purchases of £3,000.

(a) Which figure reflects the amount of VAT payable to HMRC?

	✓
£897.00	
£1,092.50	
£1,311.00	

(b) In this quarter, would the trader have more or less VAT to pay to HMRC if he was not in the flat rate scheme?

	✓
More VAT is payable not using the flat rate scheme	
More VAT is payable using the flat rate scheme	

chapter 6:
ADMINISTRATION

chapter coverage 📖

This chapter starts by determining how to deal with errors in VAT returns, depending on how large the error is, then looks at penalties that may be applied when VAT requirements are not met. The chapter then considers the effective communication of relevant VAT matters, either internally within a registered business (such as the effect on cash flow or changes in VAT legislation), with clients, or with HMRC. The topics covered are:

✍ Errors

✍ Penalties

✍ VAT and the effect on cash flow

✍ Changes in VAT legislation

✍ Contact with HMRC

✍ Maintaining up-to-date VAT knowledge

ERRORS

Introduction

A business may discover it has made an error, or errors, on a VAT return which it has already submitted.

If this is the case, the business will need to **calculate the 'net' value of all errors found relating to returns that have already been submitted**. The net error is any under-declaration of VAT less any over-declaration of VAT.

Any deliberate errors should not be included as they must be disclosed separately. They must be reported to the relevant HMRC VAT Error Correction Team, in writing and preferably using Form VAT 652 'Notification of Errors in VAT Returns', however simply writing a letter is also acceptable.

Errors exceeding the 'error correction reporting threshold'

If the net error was **not deliberate**, but is more than the greater of:

- £10,000 or

- 1% of turnover as per box 6 of the relevant return (subject to an overall £50,000 limit),

it will exceed the **error correction reporting threshold** and **cannot be adjusted for on the next VAT return.**

Instead the relevant HMRC VAT Error Correction Team must be informed in the same way as disclosing deliberate errors above.

The time limit for adjusting returns and correcting errors is **four years** from the end of the VAT period.

Task 1

A business has turnover of £6.5 million. The output tax on its last VAT return was understated by £52,000. Tick ONE statement below.

	✓
A correction can be made on the next VAT return as the error is less than 1% of turnover	
A correction cannot be made on the next return as the error exceeds £10,000	
A correction cannot be made on the next return as the error exceeds £50,000	

Errors below the 'error correction reporting threshold'

If the 'net' error (not deliberate) is below the error correction reporting threshold, **corrections can be made on the next return.**

For example:

- An understatement of output VAT on a previous return can be shown as an increase in the output tax on **box 1** of the current return.

- An overstatement of input VAT on a previous return can be shown as a decrease in the input tax on **box 4** of the current return.

Where more than one error has been made, a single correction is made being the total of all errors made in the previous return.

- If the **net effect** of all the errors is that **input VAT was overstated** on a previous return then the amount to be included as input tax on **box 4** of the current return should be reduced accordingly.

- If the **net effect** of all the errors is that **output VAT was overstated** on a previous return then the amount to be included as output tax on **box 1** of the current return should be reduced accordingly.

HOW IT WORKS

A business recorded a credit note issued to a customer as showing VAT of £60.00 instead of the correct amount of £6.00. In the same VAT period, the business included a sales invoice with VAT of £300 twice in the sales day book.

The net error is:

	£
Output tax understated by £60.00 - £6.00	54.00
Output tax overstated by £300.00	(300.00)
Net error (overstatement of output tax)	246.00

Output tax in box 1 in the next VAT return should be reduced by £246.00 to correct this error.

As we saw in Chapter 4, the VAT account should reflect the value of any adjustments made for errors.

Errors below the error correction reporting threshold do not **have** to be corrected on the net VAT return. Separate disclosure to the VAT Error Correction Team can be used instead. If this is done, the business should not also make adjustment for the same error on a later VAT return.

Task 2

A business made a 'small' overstatement of input tax on a previous return. What effect will this have on the current VAT payable to HMRC?

	✓
An increase in the VAT payable via the current return	
A decrease in the VAT payable via the current return	
No impact on the current return. It must just be separately declared	

Task 3

A business made a 'small' understatement of output tax on a previous return. Should this adjustment be shown on the latest VAT return, and if so, where on the return?

	✓
No – not shown on the return	
Yes – shown in box 1	
Yes – shown in box 4	

PENALTIES

Penalties for careless and deliberate errors

Careless and deliberate errors will be liable to a penalty, whether they are adjusted on the VAT return or reported separately.

Where errors are made in VAT returns resulting in

- An understatement of the VAT liability, or
- A false or increased repayment of VAT,

the penalty applied is likely to be the civil penalty of 'penalty for errors'.

If an error is neither careless (not taken reasonable care in making the return) nor deliberate, HMRC will expect steps to be taken to correct it, otherwise the error will be treated as careless and a penalty will arise.

Penalty for inaccurate VAT return

A penalty can arise if a VAT return is inaccurate such that it understates VAT due. It is possible to reduce this penalty, in some cases to zero, if the trader tells HMRC about inaccuracies as soon as he is aware of them.

Late VAT return or VAT payment

If a business does not submit a VAT return or pay over any VAT due by the due date, then that trader is in **default** and a **surcharge liability notice** (SLN) will be served.

The notice specifies a **surcharge period of 12 months**. If there is default involving the late payment of VAT (as opposed to simply a late return) within the surcharge period, then a surcharge is levied. This is a percentage of the unpaid VAT.

If the business does not send in a VAT return, then the amount of VAT owed will be estimated by HMRC (assessed) and the surcharge will be based upon this assessment.

Assessments

A VAT-registered business is legally obliged to submit a VAT return and pay any VAT owing by the due date.

If a return is not submitted, HMRC can raise an assessment based on what it believes is owed. If the business fails to notify HMRC within 30 days that the amount owing is actually greater than the amount assessed, the business may be liable to a penalty.

Failure to register for VAT

A penalty can be raised for failure to notify HMRC of the liability to register by the proper date.

Failure to keep and retain records

As mentioned in Chapter 3, records should be retained for **six years** for VAT purposes, unless an agreement is reached with HMRC to dispose of them earlier.

Where records have not been retained for this period, a penalty could be imposed.

Fraudulent evasion of VAT

Tax evasion consists of seeking to pay too little tax by deliberately misleading HMRC by suppressing information or providing it with false information. **Tax evasion is illegal,** as opposed to **tax avoidance**, which is more difficult to define, but broadly speaking is **any legal method of reducing your tax burden.**

Evasion of VAT includes falsely:

- Reclaiming input tax/understating output tax
- Obtaining bad debt relief
- Obtaining a repayment

Tax evasion is a criminal offence, but HMRC prefers to settle minor cases out of court with the payment of penalties and interest. HMRC will encourage cooperation and may reduce the penalty accordingly.

Extreme cases of tax evasion might result in fines and/or imprisonment.

VAT AND THE EFFECT ON CASHFLOW

We saw in Chapter 4 that the VAT return, along with the payment is (generally) due seven calendar days after the end of the month following the end of the return period.

VAT can be a substantial payment for a business to make. Provision should therefore be made to ensure that cash is reserved to pay the VAT after each period.

The person responsible for preparing the VAT return must:

- Set timescales for information to be provided to them on a timely basis

- Ensure that they have sufficient time to prepare the return before the deadline

- Contact the person responsible for paying the VAT to ensure that payment is made by the due date.

Communication of VAT amounts and due dates may also be required within an organisation as part of the preparation of the organisation's financial or cash flow forecasts.

An organisation may not need to make a VAT payment, but instead may be due a repayment of VAT. The amount and timing of this repayment is equally important for an organisation to know, so that they can manage their cash flow accordingly.

Assessment focus

There will always be a communication task within the assessment (Task 8). You may be asked to communicate payment information including amounts and time limits to a colleague within your organisation or to a client. This may be by email or internal memo.

Task 4

VAT account

Date 20XX	Reference	Debit £	Date 20XX	Reference	Credit £
1.1-31.3	Sales returns day book	474.80	1.1-31.3	Sales day book	10,422.20
1.1-31.3	Purchases day book	3,596.00	1.1-31.3	Cash book – UK sales	2,069.00
31.3	*Bad debt relief*	*195.00*	1.1-31.3	Purchases returns day book – UK purchases	204.00
31.3	*EU acquisition reclaim*	*651.20*	31.3	*Fuel scale charge*	*28.83*
31.3	BALANCE b/d	8,458.23	31.3	*EU acquisition charge*	*651.20*
	Total	**13,375.23**		**Total**	**13,375.23**
				VAT payable	8,458.23

Following on from the example in Chapter 4, use the above VAT account to complete the email below.

To: Finance Director
From: Accounting Technician
Date: 25 April 20XX
Subject: VAT return to 31 March 20XX

Please be advised that I have now completed the VAT return for the quarter to 31 March 20XX. If you are in agreement with the figures shown in the return please could you arrange an electronic payment of
£ [   ] to be made by [▼] (1)

If you wish to discuss this further please feel free to call me.

Kind regards

Picklist:
(1)   30 April 20XX / 7 May 20XX / 7 June 20XX

CHANGES IN VAT LEGISLATION

Changes in VAT legislation are usually notified by HMRC to traders via bulletins or notices. If a change affects a certain sector of businesses, then the relevant businesses will receive a paper or email version of the notice.

Changes in VAT legislation may include changes to the standard rate of VAT, changes to how certain goods are classified (eg as standard-rated, zero-rated or exempt supplies), changes to the registration and deregistration threshold (which generally occur every year) and other changes.

For the purpose of this assessment, you only need to know the rates, thresholds etc, as covered in this text and in the reference material. However, in the communication task, the assessor may pretend there has been a change in the VAT legislation, and you may be expected to draft an internal memo or email to advise relevant members of staff within an organisation. Fictional changes in VAT rate are particularly important in the assessment.

There has not been a change in VAT rates since 4 January 2011, when there was a change in the standard rate from 17.5% to 20%.

A change in the standard rate of VAT affects all VAT-registered businesses.

A change in the VAT rate will mean that from a certain date a different amount of VAT must be charged on certain supplies. In most situations this is fixed by the tax point.

HOW IT WORKS

For example, when the standard rate of VAT changed from 17.5% to 20% on 4 January 2011, a standard-rated supply of £1,000 (excluding VAT) gave rise to an invoice total of £1,175 if the tax point was before 4 January 2011, but £1,200 if the tax point was on or after 4 January 2011.

The business still only receives £1,000 after paying over the output tax to HMRC.

Assessment focus

For the purpose of your assessment you should always use 20% as the standard rate of VAT. However, you need an awareness of how a fictional change in rate (or other change in VAT legislation) can impact on businesses.

Impact on accounting systems and internal staff

A change in VAT legislation, such as a change in VAT rate, may require the **accounting systems to be adjusted.**

Where a business has a **computerised accounting system/tills** this can give rise to problems. The systems will be set to calculate VAT at a set percentage for certain supplies. In these circumstances it is usual for the company that developed the software package to give instructions as to how the VAT rate can be changed on the system.

A business's IT team should therefore be informed of the rate change to make sure that they implement these changes to the computer system.

If a **manual system is in use**, the trader simply needs to ensure that they are careful about applying the correct VAT rate for the tax point of each particular supply.

Therefore, **sales ledger and purchase ledger staff** should be informed to ensure invoices reflect the correct rate of VAT, remembering the rate of VAT must be relevant to the tax point, and not necessarily the invoice date.

A change in legislation may affect the actual price at which sales are made (if there are changes to the output VAT charged). See 'impact on customers' below. This is the case if there is a change of rate, therefore the **sales team** and **marketing team** within a business should be informed of the change.

Impact on customers

If customers are VAT-registered then they should also be aware of changes in legislation, especially with something as significant as a change in VAT rates.

However, where customers are not VAT-registered, for example in a retail business, notice should be given to customers about changes in rates.

In a retail environment this would usually be via notices displayed around the store. A change in rate could impact on the charge to the customer.

HOW IT WORKS

Using the earlier example, an item costing a customer £1,175 on 3 January 2011 would cost £1,200 on 4 January 2011 if the trader intends to **keep the same VAT-exclusive price.**

An alternative is for the trader to **keep the same VAT-inclusive price** so that there is no impact on his customers.

However, for an increase in VAT rate, this will reduce the trader's overall turnover as a greater proportion of this price charged will have to be paid to HMRC as output VAT.

Task 5

Doug is a retailer and has been selling goods to the general public for £235 (VAT-inclusive) while the VAT rate was 17.5%. (VAT fraction 7/47). When the VAT rate changed to 20% he did not want to change the cost of these goods to his customers who are not VAT-registered.

Work out for Doug the VAT-exclusive amount of the goods sold both before and after the change in the VAT rate.

VAT-inclusive £	VAT rate	VAT-exclusive £
235.00	17.5%	
235.00	20%	

CONTACT WITH HMRC

In addition to the legislation, advice about VAT rules and regulations is given in HMRC guidance. We look at how to keep your VAT knowledge up-to-date using this and other sources later in this chapter, but here we look at what to do if you need to communicate with HMRC regarding a specific VAT query.

HMRC website

If a trader has a query or problem the first step would be to check the HMRC website (www.hmrc.gov.uk).

From the homepage, 'contact us' leads you to the VAT helpline for businesses and corporations.

The HMRC website is an extremely good source of reference material for VAT, with information clearly presented to help businesses comply with regulations.

The website also contains VAT 700 **'The VAT Guide'**, which provides a business with all the information it needs about accounting for, recording and paying over VAT.

HMRC usually expect taxpayers to find answers to any queries or problems on their website. A taxpayer with a question should therefore:

- Firstly, **check the HMRC website** for the answer.

- Secondly, **telephone the VAT helpline** (with VAT registration number (if registered) and postcode).

- Finally, **write to HMRC**. It is strongly recommended that questions about VAT are sent by email, with only particularly long ones, or those where something needs to be attached, being sent by post.

It is advisable however, to get written confirmation from HMRC about issues on which doubt may arise as to the correct VAT treatment. HMRC may be reluctant to do this, but it is important so that your business (or the client you are advising) has certainty, and does not make a costly error.

Whenever a VAT-registered person contacts HMRC in writing or by telephone they should always:

- Quote their name, address, telephone number and the VAT registration number of the business

- Keep a note of the conversation and the call reference given.

The Business Link website (www.businesslink.gov.uk) is also a very useful source of VAT reference material. Business Link is a body set up by the government to provide guidance and support to businesses.

Assessment focus

In assessments, you may be required to seek guidance from HMRC in writing on some aspect of the organisation's affairs. The area that you have to enquire about may be very simple or it may be more complicated or obscure. If it is a simple point, then the task may require a brief explanation of the point as well as seeking more detailed guidance from HMRC. If the point is more complex then you will only be required to ask for guidance in an intelligent and professional manner, not to understand the sometimes complex provisions of VAT law.

Whenever contact is made with HMRC officers this must always be done in a polite and professional manner. Similarly, a professional approach should also be adopted with clients and other colleagues.

Control visits from HMRC

From time to time an HMRC officer will visit a VAT-registered business (a 'control visit') to determine whether their VAT records are correct and up to date. They are entitled to:

- Question the **business owner** or the **person responsible for keeping VAT records**

- Examine business records

- Check the correct amount of VAT has been paid or reclaimed

- Watch business activity

The following details will be confirmed in writing before the visit (unless the time before does not allow it):

- The person the officer wants to see
- A mutually agreeable date and time
- Name and contact number of visiting officer
- Which records will be examined (and for which period)
- Likely length of visit
- Any queries from the taxpayer, so the officer can prepare for them

Seven days' notice will almost always be given, unless the trader requests it earlier.

If the officer believes that VAT has been underpaid, HMRC will raise an assessment requesting payment of the VAT due. If the trader disagrees with the assessment, an appeals procedure is in place to deal with the dispute.

MAINTAINING UP-TO-DATE VAT KNOWLEDGE

As discussed earlier in this chapter, VAT rules, like those for other taxes, can frequently change. Usually there is a set timescale for when certain changes must be applied. If you are to keep your business or your clients compliant with VAT laws and practices, and so avoid surcharges and penalties, you will need to stay up-to-date with relevant information.

The assessment may include tasks testing that you know how to maintain an up-to-date knowledge of changes.

We have already seen some sources of VAT information, in particular those produced by HMRC but there are other sources.

In particular, information about **legislation changes** can be found:

- On the HMRC and other government websites
- In direct communications with businesses by HMRC
- In technical circulars in accountancy firms
- In specialist journals

Changes in practice may be identified by:

- Attending CPD updates (see below)
- Reading relevant journals
- Meeting other professionals

After you have completed your formal studies, it is important to take part in CPD (Continuing Professional Development), which may take many forms including seminars, individual research and courses. The AAT website has a separate section 'AAT CPD Interactive' for you to use. This way you will be able to keep up-to-date with VAT rules and practices, and will be able to perform your work competently and confidently.

Don't forget, much of the information covered in this chapter is available to view throughout the live assessment within the detailed reference material. Turn to the back of the text and try to identify the areas covered within this chapter.

They include:

- Errors in previous VAT returns
- Surcharges, penalties and assessments
- Finding out more information about VAT
- Visits by VAT officers

The information included in this chapter will typically be tested in the following tasks:

Task 4 **Detailed VAT rules, surcharges, penalties, corrections**

Task 8 **Communicating VAT information**

The assessor's recent comments relevant to this chapter are summarised as follows:

Knowledge of penalties and the application of them seem to be fine, however combinations of surcharges and penalties could be completed better.

When a task covers issues such as the specific deadlines for returns and payments and then the penalties for non-compliance there are some distinct problems. Students need to study the texts and legislation to ensure they know the rules because the penalties for businesses can be quite significant.

The assessor also commented on tasks which explore knowledge of errors and error correction.

Generally students need to understand that much more in-depth knowledge is needed in these areas.

Since these tasks test knowledge of the correct treatment of errors, both the AAT and training providers ought to be concerned about how much students struggle with them. In all walks of life, errors will be made and whilst this ought to be accepted, the correct approach to correcting those errors is of critical importance in most professions.

If we add the level of penalty which can be imposed for failures to correct VAT errors correctly and within the timescales laid down it becomes clear that we need to ensure students can perform much better in such a task.

Take, for example, the situation where two errors are posed and the net effect of the two has to be computed, say where a purchase invoice which included an amount of VAT has been omitted and in addition VAT from a credit note has been significantly overstated.

It is important to consider what took place originally when the error occurred and what it now means to make the adjustments. With an understated recovery and an overstated reduction in recovery the net result is to add the two errors together. Students who do not read the information carefully will not be able to make the necessary connections and hence will record an incorrect value for the correction and this happened in many cases.

The assessor's comments on the communication task included:

Accounting Technicians are not only expected to complete computations and file accounts correctly and on time, they must also be able to effectively communicate information about this work to others. In many cases this will be internal information and communications within the business, however, on occasions this will involve external communications with, for example, HM Revenue & Customs.

This task goes some way to testing that skill.

Generally this task is performed very well.

A common error however, is where students fail to notice that the business is due a VAT refund instead of the normal payment to be made to HM Revenue & Customs. Following on from that some students then fail to provide the correct information to their colleagues.

CHAPTER OVERVIEW

- If a net error exceeding the error correction reporting threshold is discovered from a previous tax period, it cannot be adjusted in the VAT return. Instead voluntary disclosure should be made and the HMRC VAT Error Correction Team informed. A penalty might be imposed depending on the behaviour of the business.

- If a VAT return or payment is late, the taxpayer is served with a surcharge liability notice and may have a surcharge to pay if further payment defaults occur.

- A number of other penalties apply for VAT purposes including failure to register and failure to keep records.

- VAT evasion is a criminal offence and may give rise to fines and/or imprisonment.

- VAT can be a substantial payment for a business. Therefore steps must be taken to ensure both the return and payment can be made by the due dates.

- Changes in VAT legislation can have significant impact on accounting systems.

- Staff and customers need to be informed of a change to the VAT rate.

- HMRC expect taxpayers to try and resolve any queries by checking their website before telephoning or writing to them. However sometimes written confirmation about an issue should be insisted upon.

- HMRC officers may from time to time visit a VAT-registered business to check on VAT records.

- It is important to maintain up-to-date knowledge of changes to VAT legislation and practice.

Keywords

Error correction reporting threshold – this is the threshold that dictates whether errors discovered on a previous return can be corrected on the next return or must be reported separately

Surcharge liability notice – this warns a business that its VAT return or payment was not received on time and if the business pays late within the next 12 months, a default surcharge will be due

Voluntary disclosure – the action of notifying HMRC of any error found in previous returns

Evasion of VAT – falsely reclaiming input VAT/understating output tax, obtaining bad debt relief or obtaining a repayment

HMRC website – the first place a taxpayer must check to try and resolve any VAT queries

TEST YOUR LEARNING

Test 1

Identify which one of the following statements is correct.

	✓
If a net error of more than the lower of £10,000 and 1% of turnover (subject to an overall £5,000 limit) is discovered it must be disclosed on Form VAT 652.	
If a net error of more than the greater of £10,000 and 1% of turnover (subject to an overall £5,000 limit) is discovered it must be disclosed on Form VAT 652.	
If a net error of more than the lower of £10,000 and 1% of turnover (subject to an overall £50,000 limit) is discovered it must be disclosed on Form VAT 652.	
If a net error of more than the greater of £10,000 and 1% of turnover (subject to an overall £50,000 limit) is discovered it must be disclosed on Form VAT 652.	

Test 2

Identify whether the following statement is True or False.

Tax avoidance is illegal and could lead to fines and/or imprisonment.

True ✓	False ✓

Test 3

You are a trainee accounting technician working for a sole trader, Mr Smith. Mr Smith has just received a letter from a client, Michael James (a trader making only standard rated supplies to non VAT-registered clients) asking about the impact of a recent change in the standard rate of VAT on his clients. The rate changed from 20% to 25%. He is undecided about whether to change his prices.

You are required to complete the following letter to Michael James discussing the options open to him.

Mr Smith
Number Street
London
SW11 8AB

Mr James
Alphabet Street
London
W12 6WM

Dear Mr James

CHANGE IN THE STANDARD RATE OF VAT

Further to your recent letter, I have set out below the options open to you in relation to the standard rate of VAT.

Until recently you have been charging VAT at a rate of [_____] ▼ (1) Therefore a VAT-exclusive sale with a value of £1,000 has cost your non VAT-registered clients £ [_____] ▼ (2) £1,000 plus VAT.

The two options open to you are as follows:

- Keep the same VAT-exclusive value of £1,000

  The benefit of this option is that you have the same amount of VAT-exclusive sales value per item sold. However, this will now make the VAT-inclusive cost to your customers higher at [_____] ▼ (3). This may make your prices less competitive (if your competitors do not do the same) and may result in a loss of some customers.

- Keep the same VAT-inclusive value of £ [_____] ▼ (4)

  Under this alternative option you will remain competitive to your customers. However, your VAT-exclusive sales value per item sold will be reduced to [_____] ▼ (5).

There is no obvious correct option to choose, it will depend primarily on the strength of your competitors.

If you wish to discuss this with me in more detail please do not hesitate to contact me.

Your sincerely

Mr Smith

Picklists:

(1)   10% / 20% / 25%
(2)   1,000 / 1,200 / 1,250
(3)   £1,000 / £1,200 (£1,000 plus VAT at 20%) / £1,250 (£1,000 plus VAT at 25%)
(4)   1,000 / 1,200 / 1,250
(5)   £1,000 (£1,200 × 100/120) / £960 (£1,200 × 100/125)

Test 4

A taxpayer should try and resolve a VAT query in the following order:

(Fill in the blank space from the pick list below)

Firstly...	▼
If no luck, then...	▼
Still cannot resolve, then...	▼

Picklist:

- Write to or email HMRC
- Check HMRC website
- Ring the HMRC VAT helpline

Test 5

Identify which one of the following statements is correct.

	✓
A VAT officer will usually turn up for a control visit unannounced.	
A VAT officer can check the correct amount of VAT has been paid or reclaimed.	
A VAT officer is not entitled to examine the business records.	

ANSWERS TO CHAPTER TASKS

CHAPTER 1   VAT basics

Task 1

	Input tax ✓	Output tax ✓
Business A		✓
Business B	✓	

Task 2

The correct answers are:

Business type	Type of supply made	Net cost £
Insurance company	Only exempt supplies	1,200
Accountancy firm	Only standard-rated supplies	1,000
Bus company	Only zero-rated supplies	1,000

Although the accountancy firm and bus company pay £1,200 for their telephone bills, they are able to reclaim the input VAT of £200, so the net cost is £1,000. The insurance company making exempt supplies is not able to reclaim input tax and so the net cost is £1,200.

Task 3

Amy will exceed the threshold by 30 April 2016.

Amy must therefore register for VAT by 30 May 2016 (within 30 days).

VAT registration is required when TAXABLE supplies (standard plus zero-rated supplies) exceed £82,000. Taxable supplies are £9,120 (£7,850 + £1,270) per month.

Amy exceeds this threshold after 9 months, ie by 30 April 2016 as taxable supplies are then £82,080 (9 × £9,120).

Task 4

	✓
At the beginning of month 12, Richard expects his taxable supplies will exceed £82,000 in the next 30 days.	
At the end of month 12, Richard's taxable supplies in the previous 12 months have exceeded £82,000.	✓

The historic test is met at the end of month 12.

For the future test to be met, the taxable supplies in the next 30 days **alone** must exceed the threshold, ie the taxable supplies in the previous 11 months are not included. Therefore, the future test is not met here.

Task 5

	✓
Preparation of VAT returns would be optional.	
Customers would benefit by being able to claim back input VAT.	
Business would benefit by being able to claim back input VAT.	✓

Once registered, even voluntarily, VAT returns will have to be completed.

VAT-registered customers would neither gain nor lose because they could reclaim VAT charged to them, and non VAT-registered customers would be disadvantaged because they would be charged VAT they could not reclaim.

CHAPTER 2   Inputs and outputs

Task 1

Net £	VAT rate %	VAT £	Gross £
43.50	20	8.70	52.20
18.00	20	3.60	21.60

VAT = £52.20 × 1/6   VAT = £18.00 × 20%

  = £8.70   = £3.60

Task 2

Circumstance	Yes, can reclaim ✓	No, cannot reclaim ✓
Input tax incurred entertaining prospective new UK client		✓
Input tax incurred on a new car for the top salesperson		✓
Input tax incurred on a car for use in a driving instruction business	✓	

Task 3

	True ✓	False ✓
A VAT-registered business can reclaim all the input VAT on road fuel if it keeps detailed records of business and private mileage, and makes no other adjustment.		✓
A VAT-registered business can reclaim all the input VAT on road fuel if it pays the appropriate fuel scale charge for private mileage.	✓	

Task 4

	True ✓	False ✓
A VAT-registered business can reclaim all the input VAT attributed to zero-rated supplies.	✓	
A VAT-registered business can reclaim all the input VAT attributed to standard-rated supplies	✓	
A VAT-registered business can reclaim all the input VAT attributed to exempt supplies		✓
A VAT-registered business can reclaim all the input VAT attributed to both taxable and exempt supplies providing certain de minimis tests are satisfied	✓	

Task 5

To VAT-registered traders	To non VAT-registered traders	✓
Zero-rated	Zero-rated	
Standard-rated	Zero-rated	
Zero-rated	Standard-rated	✓
Standard-rated	Standard-rated	

Task 6

	✓
No VAT is charged by the EU supplier therefore can be ignored by Joe on his VAT return.	
Joe must pay output VAT to HMRC at the port/airport and can reclaim input VAT on the next return.	
Joe must charge himself 'output VAT' and 'reclaim input' VAT on the same return.	✓

CHAPTER 3   Accounting for VAT

Task 1

	✓
Customer VAT registration number	
Supplier VAT registration number	✓
Total VAT-exclusive amount for each type of item sold	✓
Total VAT amount for each type of item sold	✓
Total VAT-inclusive amount for each type of item sold	

Task 2

	✓
Input tax will increase	✓
Input tax will decrease	
Output tax will increase	
Output tax will decrease	

Task 3

	True ✓	False ✓
A 'simplified' invoice can be used to reclaim input VAT	✓	
A 'pro forma' invoice can be used to reclaim input VAT		✓

Task 4

	✓
Input tax will increase	
Input tax will decrease	
Output tax will increase	
Output tax will decrease	✓

Task 5

	✓
15 May 20X0	
20 May 20X0	✓
20 June 20X0	

Basic tax point	15 May 20X0
Invoice date	20 May 20X0
Payment date	20 June 20X0
Is payment or invoice earlier than basic tax point?	No – so this does not create an actual tax point
Is invoice within 14 days of basic tax point?	Yes – so invoice date over-rides basic tax point
TAX POINT	**20 May – actual**

Task 6

	✓
2 June 20X0	✓
11 June 20X0	✓
29 June 20X0	
31 July 20X0	

Tax point

	10% deposit	*Balancing payment*
Basic tax point	11 June 20X0	11 June 20X0
Invoice date	29 June 20X0	29 June 20X0
Payment date	2 June 20X0	31 July 20X0
Is payment or invoice earlier than basic tax point?	Yes – payment 2 June 20X0	No – both later
Is invoice within 14 days of basic tax point?	No	No
TAX POINT	2 June – actual	11 June – basic

Task 7

	✓
The amount payable will increase	
The amount payable will decrease	✓

CHAPTER 4   The VAT return

Task 1

	✓
£7,950	
£11,700	✓

By entering the VAT paid debit of £3,750.00, on the credit side, the balance on the account is showing as £11,700 instead of the correct £4,200.00

Date 20X0	Reference	Debit £	Date 20X0	Reference	Credit £
			31/3/X0	VAT payable	3,750.00
			31/3/X0	**VAT paid**	**3,750.00**
			30/6/X0	VAT payable	4,200.00
	Balance	11,700.00			
	Total	**11,700.00**		**Total**	**11,700.00**

Task 2

	✓
Input tax paid at the ports is reclaimed as input tax on the VAT return.	
Both input tax and output tax in relation to the goods are shown on the VAT return.	✓
They are zero-rated and so no VAT features on the VAT return.	
They are exempt and so no VAT features on the VAT return.	

Task 3

	✓
The fuel scale charge increases output VAT and is shown in Box 1.	✓
VAT on EU acquisitions increases both input VAT and output VAT and is shown in boxes 1 & 4.	
Credit notes received from suppliers reduce input VAT and are shown in box 4.	✓
Credit notes issued to customers reduce output VAT and are shown in box 1.	✓

VAT on EU acquisitions increases both input VAT and output VAT but is shown in boxes 2 and 4

Task 4

VAT return for quarter ended 31.03.20X0		£
VAT due in this period on sales and other outputs.	Box 1	6,880.00
Total value of sales and all other outputs excluding any VAT. Include your box 8 figure. Whole pounds only.	Box 6	62,450
Total value of all supplies of goods and related costs, excluding any VAT, to other EC Member States. Whole pounds only.	Box 8	18,345

Box 1 = (27,200 + 7,200) × 20%

Box 6 = 27,200 + 9,705 + 18,345 + 7,200

Box 8 = 18,345

Task 5

VAT return for quarter ended 31/3/X0		£
VAT due in this period on acquisitions from other EC Member States	Box 2	1,669.00
VAT reclaimed in this period on purchases and other inputs, including acquisitions from the EC	Box 4	3,756.00
Total value of purchases and all other inputs excluding any VAT. Include your box 9 figure. Whole pounds only	Box 7	18,780
Total value of all acquisitions of goods and related costs, excluding any VAT, from other EC Member States. Whole pounds only	Box 9	8,345

Box 2 = 8,345 × 20%

Box 4 = (9,230 + 1,205 + 8,345) × 20%

Box 7 = 9,230 + 1,205 + 8,345

Box 9 = 8,345

CHAPTER 5 Schemes for small businesses

Task 1

	True ✓	False ✓
The first payment due to HMRC is by 1 April 2015.		✓

The first payment due to HMRC is by 30 April 2015 (ie the END of month 4).

Task 2

	✓
Yes, because they would be able to reclaim input VAT earlier	
Yes, because they would pay output VAT later	
No, because they would reclaim input VAT later	✓
No, because they would pay output VAT earlier	

Task 3

	✓
£2,550	
£3,060	✓

The VAT due to HMRC is 8.5% of the VAT inclusive figure.

$(£30,000 \times 120\%) \times 8.5\% = £3,060$

CHAPTER 6 Administration

Task 1

	✓
A correction can be made on the next VAT return as the error is less than 1% of turnover.	
A correction cannot be made on the next return as the error exceeds £10,000.	
A correction cannot be made on the next return as the error exceeds £50,000.	✓

The error is less than 1% of turnover, but that is subject to an overall limit of £50,000.

Task 2

	✓
An increase in the VAT payable via the current return.	✓
A decrease in the VAT payable via the current return.	
No impact on the current return. It must just be separately declared.	

Task 3

	✓
No – not shown on the return	
Yes – shown in box 1	✓
Yes – shown in box 4	

It is shown as an increase in the output tax at box 1 on the VAT return.

Task 4

To: Finance Director
From: Accounting Technician
Date: 25 April 20XX
Subject: VAT return to 31 March 20XX

Please be advised that I have now completed the VAT return for the quarter to 31 March 20XX. If you are in agreement with the figures shown in the return please could you arrange an electronic payment of **£8,458.23** to be made by **7 May 20XX**.

If you wish to discuss this further please feel free to call me.

Kind regards

Task 5

VAT-inclusive £	VAT rate	VAT exclusive £
235.00	17.5%	200.00
235.00	20%	195.83

- VAT rate of 17.5% (VAT fraction 7/47 or 17.5/117.5)

  VAT exclusive value £235 – (7/47 × £235) = £200
- VAT rate of 20% (VAT fraction 1/6 or 20/120)

  VAT exclusive value £235 – (1/6 × £235) = £195.83

Answers to chapter tasks

TEST YOUR LEARNING – ANSWERS

CHAPTER 1   VAT basics

Test 1

	✓
HM Customs & Excise	
Inland Revenue	
HM Revenue & Customs	✓
HM Treasury	

Test 2

	✓
Output VAT is the VAT charged by a supplier on the sales that are made by his business. Output VAT is collected by the supplier and paid over to HMRC.	✓
Output VAT is the VAT suffered by the purchaser of the goods which will be reclaimed from HMRC if the purchaser is VAT-registered.	

The other statement describes input VAT.

Test 3

VAT is collected by HMRC throughout the manufacturing/supply chain for goods. Each VAT-registered business that buys, processes and then sells the goods pays the difference between the VAT on their sale and the VAT on their purchase over to HMRC.

Test 4

	True ✓	False ✓
If a business supplies zero-rated services then the business is not able to reclaim the VAT on its purchases and expenses from HMRC.		✓
A business makes zero-rated supplies. The cost to the business of its purchases and expenses is the VAT exclusive amount.	✓	

Test 5

		Register without delay	Register within 30 days	Monitor and register later
A	An existing business with total turnover for the previous 11 months of £80,000. Sales for the next month are unknown at present.			✓
B	A new business with an expected turnover for the next 12 months of £6,950 per month.			✓
C	An existing business with total turnover for the previous 12 months of £6,900 per month.		✓	

Test 6

AN Accountant
Number Street
London
SW11 8AB

Mrs Quirke
Alphabet Street
London
W12 6WM

Dear Mrs Quirke

VAT REGISTRATION

Further to our recent telephone conversation, set out below are the circumstances when you must register your business for VAT.

If the taxable turnover of your business at the end of a month, looking back no more than **twelve** months, has exceeded the registration limit of **£82,000**, then the business must apply to register for VAT within 30 days.

Alternatively, if at any time, the taxable turnover (before any VAT is added) is expected to exceed the registration limit within the next **30 days** alone, then the business must apply to be registered for VAT without delay. This would be the situation if, for example, you obtained a large additional contract for, say, £85,000.

If you wish to discuss this in any more detail please do not hesitate to contact me.

Yours sincerely

AN Accountant

CHAPTER 2 Inputs and outputs

Test 1

(a)

The VAT is £	76.80

VAT   =   £384.00 × 20%

        =   £76.80

(b)

	Output tax ✓	Input tax ✓
Business C	✓	
Business D		✓

Test 2

	✓
Staff party	
Car for sales manager	✓
Photocopier	
Entertaining UK clients	✓

Test 3

VAT-inclusive £	VAT at 20 % £
42.88	7.14
96.57	16.09
28.20	4.70
81.07	13.51

(i)	£42.88 × 1/6	=	£7.14
(ii)	£96.57 × 1/6	=	£16.09
(iii)	£28.20 × 1/6	=	£4.70
(iv)	£81.07 × 1/6	=	£13.51

Test 4

	✓
The goods will be treated as standard-rated in the UK if the American business is VAT-registered.	
The goods will be treated as standard-rated in the UK provided documentary evidence of the export is obtained within three months.	
The goods will be treated as zero-rated in the UK if the American business is VAT-registered.	
The goods will be treated as zero-rated in the UK provided documentary evidence of the export is obtained within three months.	✓

CHAPTER 3   Accounting for VAT

Test 1

	✓
1 year	
2 years	
6 years	✓
20 years	

Test 2

	✓
A pro forma invoice is always sent out when goods are sent to customers, before issuing the proper invoice	
A pro forma invoice should always include the words 'This is not a VAT invoice'	✓
A customer can reclaim VAT stated on a pro forma invoice	
A pro forma invoice is sent out to offer a customer the chance to purchase the goods detailed	✓

Test 3

	Date	Basic/ Actual
An invoice is sent out to a customer for goods on 22 June 20X0 and the goods are despatched on 29 June 20X0	22 June	A
Goods are sent out to a customer on 18 June 20X0 and this is followed by an invoice on 23 June 20X0	23 June	A
A customer pays in full for goods on 27 June 20X0 and they are then delivered to the customer on 2 July 20X0	27 June	A

Test 4

The VAT on a bad debt can be reclaimed from HMRC when the following conditions are met:

- The debt is more than six months overdue and less than four years and six months old
- The original VAT on the invoice has been paid to HMRC
- The debt is written-off in the accounts of the business
- The debt still belongs to the business

CHAPTER 4   The VAT return

Test 1

	True ✓	False ✓
If input VAT is greater than output VAT on the return, VAT is payable to HMRC		✓
If output VAT is greater than input VAT on the return, VAT is repayable from HMRC		✓

If input VAT is greater than output VAT on the return then VAT is repayable, and if output VAT is greater than input VAT on the return, then VAT is payable to HMRC.

Test 2

	✓
The payment of £4,700 for the previous quarter has been included twice in the VAT account	
The payment of £4,700 for the previous quarter has been omitted from the VAT account	✓

By omitting the VAT paid debit of £4,700.00, the balance on the account is showing as £12,220.00 instead of the correct £7,520.00

Date 20XX	Reference	Debit £	Date 20XX	Reference	Credit £
QTR 1	VAT paid		QTR 1	VAT payable	4,700.00
			QTR 2	VAT payable	7,520.00
	Balance	12,220.00			
	Total	**12,220.00**		**Total**	**12,220.00**
			QTR 2	VAT payable	12,220.00

Test 3

VAT return for quarter ended 30.6.20XX		£
VAT due in this period on **sales** and other outputs	Box 1	7,520.00
VAT due in this period on **acquisitions** from other **EC Member States**	Box 2	750.00
Total VAT due (**the sum of boxes 1 and 2**)	Box 3	8,270.00
VAT reclaimed in this period on **purchases** and other inputs, including acquisitions from the EC	Box 4	3,950.00
Net VAT to be paid to HM Revenue & Customs or reclaimed by you (**Difference between boxes 3 and 4 – if Box 4 is greater than Box 3, use a minus sign**)	Box 5	4,320.00
Total value of **sales** and all other outputs excluding any VAT. **Include your box 8 figure. Whole pounds only**	Box 6	43,400
Total value of **purchases** and all other inputs excluding any VAT. **Include your box 9 figure. Whole pounds only**	Box 7	19,250
Total value of all **supplies** of goods and related costs, excluding any VAT, to other **EC Member States. Whole pounds only**	Box 8	0
Total value of all **acquisitions** of goods and related costs, excluding any VAT, from other **EC Member States. Whole pounds only**	Box 9	3,750

Workings:

		£
Box 1	VAT on sales from the sales day book	5,200.00
	VAT on sales from the cash book	2,800.00
	Less: VAT on credit notes	(480.00)
		7,520.00
Box 2	VAT due on EU acquisitions	750.00
Box 3	Total of box 1 and box 2	
	£7,520.00 + £750.00	8,270.00
Box 4	VAT on purchases from purchases day book	3,100.00
	VAT on EU acquisitions	750.00
	Bad debt relief (£500.00 × 20%)	100.00
		3,950.00
Box 5	Net VAT due Box 3 minus box 4	
	£8,270.00 – £3,950.00	4,320.00
Box 6	Standard-rated credit UK sales	26,000.00
	Less: standard-rated credit notes	(2,400.00)
	Cash sales	14,000.00
	Exports	5,800.00
		43,400
Box 7	Standard-rated credit purchases	15,500.00
	EU acquisitions	3,750.00
		19,250
Box 8	EU sales	0
Box 9	EU acquisitions	3,750

Test 4

VAT return for quarter ended 31.5.20XX		£
VAT due in this period on **sales** and other outputs	Box 1	7,066.78
VAT due in this period on **acquisitions** from other **EC Member States**	Box 2	0
Total VAT due (**the sum of boxes 1 and 2**)	Box 3	7,066.78
VAT reclaimed in this period on **purchases** and other inputs, including acquisitions from the EC	Box 4	4,735.17
Net VAT to be paid to HM Revenue & Customs or reclaimed by you (**Difference between boxes 3 and 4 – if Box 4 is greater than Box 3, use a minus sign**)	Box 5	2,331.61
Total value of **sales** and all other outputs excluding any VAT. **Include your box 8 figure. Whole pounds only**	Box 6	38,890
Total value of **purchases** and all other inputs excluding any VAT. **Include your box 9 figure. Whole pounds only**	Box 7	26,154
Total value of all **supplies** of goods and related costs, excluding any VAT, to other **EC Member States. Whole pounds only**	Box 8	0
Total value of all **acquisitions** of goods and related costs, excluding any VAT, from other **EC Member States. Whole pounds only**	Box 9	0

Tutorial note: In past assessments, the entries for boxes 6 – 9 have been accepted whether rounded up or down to the nearest pound. However, if the task does give particular instructions on rounding, then these instructions should be followed.

Workings:

		£
Box 1	VAT on sales from the sales day book	6,135.65
	VAT on sales from the cash book	1,010.90
	Less: VAT on credit notes	(79.77)
		7,066.78
Box 2	VAT due on EU acquisitions	0
Box 3	Total of box 1 and box 2	7,066.78
Box 4	VAT on purchases from purchases day book	4,090.17
	VAT on purchases from cash payments book	606.60
	Bad debt relief	38.40
		4,735.17
Box 5	Net VAT due Box 3 minus box 4	2,331.61
Box 6	Zero-rated credit UK sales	3,581.67
	Standard-rated credit UK sales	30,678.25
	Cash sales	5,054.51
	Less: zero-rated credit notes	(25.59)
	Less: standard-rated credit notes	(398.86)
		38,890
Box 7	Zero-rated credit UK purchases	2,669.80
	Standard-rated credit UK purchases	20,450.85
	Cash purchases	3,033.01
		26,154
Box 8	EU sales	0
Box 9	EU acquisitions	0

CHAPTER 5   Schemes for small businesses

Test 1

AN accountant
Number Street
London
SW11 8AB

Mr Lymstock
Alphabet Street
London
W12 6WM

Dear Mr Lymstock

ANNUAL ACCOUNTING SCHEME

I have recently been reviewing your files. I would like to make you aware of a scheme that you could use for VAT.

As the annual value of your taxable supplies, **excluding** VAT and supplies of capital items, in the following 12 months is expected to be **no more than £1,350,000** you can join the annual accounting scheme.

Under this scheme you make **nine** monthly direct debit payments based on your VAT liability for the previous year. The first of these payments is due at the end of the **fourth** month of the accounting period. You must then prepare a VAT return for the year and submit it in with the balancing payment, by **two months** after the year end.

Use of this annual accounting scheme is a great help as it means that you only have to prepare **one** VAT return(s) each year.

If you wish to discuss this with me in more detail please do not hesitate to contact me.

Your sincerely

AN Accountant

Test 2

If the annual value of taxable supplies, **excluding** VAT, is **no more** than **£1,350,000** and provided that a trader has a clean record with HMRC, he may be able to apply to use the cash accounting scheme.

The scheme allows the accounting for VAT to be based upon the date of **receipt and payment of money**. This is particularly useful for a business which gives its customers a **long** period of credit whilst paying its suppliers promptly.

The scheme also gives automatic relief **for bad debts** so if the customer does not pay the amount due, then the VAT need not be accounted for to HMRC.

Test 3

	✓
£897.00	
£1,092.50	
£1,311.00	✓

£9,500 × 120 % × 11.5% = £1,311.00

	✓
More VAT is payable not using the flat rate scheme	
More VAT is payable using the flat rate scheme	✓

If not using the flat rate scheme the VAT payable would be:

		£
Output tax	£9,500 × 20%	1,900.00
Input tax	£3,000 × 20%	(600.00)
		1,300.00

CHAPTER 6   Administration

Test 1

The correct statement is:

	✓
If a net error of more than the lower of £10,000 and 1% of turnover (subject to an overall £5,000 limit) is discovered it must be disclosed on Form VAT 652.	
If a net error of more than the greater of £10,000 and 1% of turnover (subject to an overall £5,000 limit) is discovered it must be disclosed on Form VAT 652.	
If a net error of more than the lower of £10,000 and 1% of turnover (subject to an overall £50,000 limit) is discovered it must be disclosed on Form VAT 652.	
If a net error of more than the greater of £10,000 and 1% of turnover (subject to an overall £50,000 limit) is discovered it must be disclosed on Form VAT 652.	✓

Test 2

True	False
✓	✓
	✓

Tax **evasion** is illegal and could lead to fines and/or imprisonment, as opposed to tax **avoidance.**

Test 3

Mr Smith
Number Street
London
SW11 8AB

Mr James
Alphabet Street
London
W12 6WM

Dear Mr James

CHANGE IN THE STANDARD RATE OF VAT

Further to your recent letter, I have set out below the options open to you in relation to the standard rate of VAT.

Until recently you have been charging VAT at a rate of **20%**. Therefore a VAT-exclusive sale with a value of £1,000 has cost your non VAT-registered clients **£1,200** (£1,000 plus VAT).

The two options open to you are as follows:

- Keep the same VAT-exclusive value of £1,000

    The benefit of this option is that you have the same amount of VAT-exclusive sales value per item sold. However, this will now make the VAT-inclusive cost to your customers higher at **£1,250 (£1,000 plus VAT at 25%)**. This may make your prices less competitive (if your competitors do not do the same) and may result in a loss of some customers.

- Keep the same VAT-inclusive value of £**1,200**

    Under this alternative option you will remain competitive to your customers. However, your VAT-exclusive sales value per item sold will be reduced to **£960.00 (£1,200 × 100/125)**.

There is no obvious correct option to choose, it will depend primarily on the strength of your competitors.

If you wish to discuss this with me in more detail please do not hesitate to contact me.

Your sincerely

Mr Smith

Test 4

A taxpayer should try and resolve a VAT query in the following order:

Firstly...	Check HMRC website
If no luck, then...	Ring the HMRC VAT helpline
Still cannot resolve, then...	Write to or email HMRC

Test 5

	✓
A VAT officer will usually turn up for a control visit unannounced	
A VAT officer can check the correct amount of VAT has been paid or reclaimed	✓
A VAT officer is not entitled to examine the business records	

Question bank

Indirect Tax Question Bank

Chapter 1 – VAT basics

Task 1.1

Black Ltd, a VAT-registered business, pays for goods from a supplier, and the amount includes VAT.

Is this amount of VAT to be treated as output VAT or input VAT for Black Ltd?

TICK ONE BOX.

Output tax	
Input tax	

Task 1.2

A VAT-registered retailer buys a product for £100 plus VAT of £20. The retailer sells the product to a member of the public for £125 plus VAT of £25.

Which of the following statements is TRUE?

TICK ONE BOX.

	✓
The retailer suffers a net cost of £5 VAT being the difference between its output and input tax on the product.	
The true cost of the product to the retailer is £120.	
The retailer does not bear any of the cost of VAT. The member of the public bears the full cost of £25 VAT.	
The retailer bears a VAT cost of £20 and the member of the public bears a VAT cost of £25.	

Task 1.3

A trader buys a product from a manufacturer for £200 plus VAT of £40. The trader is not VAT-registered. The trader sells the product to a member of the public.

Which of the following statements is TRUE?

TICK ONE BOX.

	✓
The true cost of the product to the trader is £200.	
The trader suffers a VAT cost of £40.	
The trader accounts for output VAT of £40 on its purchase from the manufacturer.	
The member of the public suffers a VAT cost of £40.	

Task 1.4

Identify which of the following types of supply are deemed to be taxable supplies for VAT purposes.

TICK ONE BOX.

	✓
Standard-rated supplies only	
Standard and zero-rated supplies	
Zero-rated and exempt supplies	
All three types of supply	

Task 1.5

Several businesses each purchased goods during a month for £13,500 plus VAT.

Identify whether each of these businesses would be able to reclaim the input tax on the goods purchased.

TICK ONE BOX FOR EACH BUSINESS.

Business	Yes, can reclaim ✓	No, cannot reclaim ✓
Bread Ltd – making only standard-rated supplies		
Soup Ltd – making only exempt supplies		
Marmalade Ltd – making only zero-rated supplies		

Task 1.6

A VAT-registered business making only zero-rated supplies has just paid £100 plus VAT of £20 for goods.

What is the net cost of the goods to the business?

TICK ONE BOX.

Cost	✓
£0	
£20	
£100	
£120	

Task 1.7

Jam Ltd is a bus company making only zero-rated supplies.

Which ONE of the following statements is correct in relation to Jam Ltd?

TICK ONE BOX.

	Correct ✓
Jam Ltd cannot register for VAT	
If Jam Ltd is VAT-registered it will make payments to HMRC	
If Jam Ltd is VAT-registered it will have repayments from HMRC	

Task 1.8

Bradley's business makes taxable supplies of approximately £30,000 each year. He is considering voluntarily registering for VAT.

Identify whether the following statements are true or false in relation to voluntary registration.

TICK ONE BOX FOR EACH STATEMENT.

	True	False
If Bradley's business makes zero-rated supplies, it will be in a VAT repayment position		
If Bradley makes standard-rated supplies, it could be disadvantageous for non VAT-registered customers		

Task 1.9

Identify whether the following businesses making taxable supplies need to register for VAT immediately, within the next 30 days, or monitor turnover and perhaps register later.

TICK ONE BOX ON EACH LINE.

	Register now	Register within 30 days	Monitor and register later
An existing business with a total turnover of £6,650 per month for the last 12 months			
A new business with an expected turnover of £25,000 per month for the next 12 months			
An existing business with a total turnover of £6,000 per month for the last 12 months. A new contract will bring in additional sales of £83,000 in ten days time			

Task 1.10

Identify whether each of these businesses can register for VAT.

TICK ONE BOX FOR EACH BUSINESS.

	Can register	Cannot register
Blackberry Ltd – making only zero-rated supplies		
Raspberry Ltd – making standard-rated and zero-rated supplies		
Loganberry Ltd – making only exempt supplies		
Gooseberry Ltd – making standard-rated and exempt supplies		

Task 1.11

Flan Ltd makes only zero-rated supplies.

Identify whether the following statements are True or False in relation to VAT registration.

TICK ONE BOX FOR EACH STATEMENT.

	True	False
Flan Ltd cannot register for VAT as it makes only zero-rated supplies		
Flan Ltd is automatically exempt from registering for VAT		
Flan Ltd can register for VAT		
Flan Ltd can apply to HMRC to be exempt from registration		

Task 1.12

Identify whether the following supplies are included when considering whether the VAT registration limit has been reached.

TICK ONE BOX ON EACH LINE.

	Include	Exclude
Standard-rated supplies		
Zero-rated supplies		
Exempt supplies		

Task 1.13

A VAT-registered trader's sales are looking like they will fall below the deregistration limit.

Complete the sentence below by selecting the appropriate number.

The trader may deregister if:

Taxable turnover in the next	▼	months is expected to fall below the deregistration limit.

Picklist:

3 / 12 / 24

Task 1.14

The deregistration threshold (for the purpose of your assessment) is:

TICK ONE BOX.

	✓
£80,000	
£82,000	
£150,000	
£1.35 million	

....

Task 1.15

A business has exceeded the VAT registration limit in the last 12 months for the first time. However, this was because of one unusual contract which is unlikely to be repeated.

Identify whether the following statement is True or False.

TICK ONE BOX.

	True	False
The business can apply to HMRC for exception from registration, because the level of taxable supplies was temporary.		

....

Chapter 2 – Inputs and outputs

Task 2.1

Below are details of two VAT invoices to be issued by a trader who makes only standard-rated supplies.

Insert the figures in the relevant columns, as appropriate.

Invoice number	Net £	VAT £	Gross £
1000325			390.60
1000326	452.92		

. . . .

Task 2.2

Identify whether input tax can be reclaimed by a VAT-registered business in each of the following circumstances.

TICK ONE BOX ON EACH LINE.

Circumstance	Yes, can reclaim ✓	No, cannot reclaim ✓
Input tax incurred entertaining a UK client (meals provided during a meeting)		
Input tax incurred on the purchase of a van for use by a furniture repair business		
Input tax incurred providing meals on a training course for an employee		

. . . .

Task 2.3

Dish Ltd, a VAT-registered business, purchases all of the fuel for cars used by the salesmen. The company reclaims the VAT on the fuel purchased. The salesmen also use the cars for private motoring.

Complete the sentence below by selecting the appropriate word.

On the VAT return Dish Ltd must include an amount of	▼	tax to take
account of the private fuel used by salesmen		

Picklist:

output
input

....

Task 2.4

A VAT-registered business has made the following purchases:

- A car for use by the sales manager for £14,200 plus VAT
- A van for use by the stores man for £10,500 plus VAT

Identify how much VAT can be reclaimed by the business?

TICK ONE BOX.

	✓
Nil	
£2,840.00	
£2,100.00	
£4,940.00	

....

Task 2.5

Where a VAT-registered business makes a mixture of standard-rated, zero-rated and exempt supplies, which of the following statements is correct?

TICK ONE BOX.

	✓
All input tax can be reclaimed	
Only input tax relating to standard-rated supplies can be reclaimed	
All input tax can be reclaimed provided certain de minimis tests are met	
Only input tax relating to standard and zero-rated supplies can be reclaimed	
No input tax can be reclaimed	

Task 2.6

Mohammed has purchased goods from a supplier in another EU country.

Complete the sentence below by selecting the appropriate word.

This purchase is known as an/a	▼

Picklist:

import
export
acquisition
despatch

Task 2.7

James is VAT-registered and is selling goods to a VAT-registered trader in another EU country.

Complete the sentence below by selecting the appropriate word(s).

In order to benefit from zero rating the customer must provide	▼

Picklist:

nothing
his EU VAT-registration number
his name and business address
evidence of receipt of goods

Task 2.8

Lucinda is VAT-registered and is selling goods to a customer in India, which is outside the EU.

Complete the sentence below by selecting the appropriate word(s).

Goods exported to customers outside the EU must be treated as	▼

Picklist:

outside the scope of VAT
standard-rated
zero-rated
exempt

Task 2.9

Jones Ltd, a VAT-registered business which makes standard-rated supplies, imports goods from outside the EU. The imported goods would be standard-rated with VAT of £3,100 if supplied in the UK.

Which one of the following is the net VAT position for Jones Ltd?

TICK ONE BOX.

	Correct
VAT payable to HMRC of £3,100	
VAT reclaimed from HMRC of £3,100	
Nil net VAT effect	

Task 2.10

A UK VAT-registered business acquires goods from a VAT-registered supplier in another EU country.

Which ONE of the following statements is correct?

TICK ONE BOX.

	✓
As long as the UK business supplies its VAT number to the EU supplier the goods will be zero-rated and VAT doesn't need to be accounted for	
The UK business will charge itself output tax for the goods on the VAT return and reclaim input tax on the same return	
The UK business will pay output tax to HMRC at the point of entry into the UK and reclaim input tax on the next return	
The EU supplier will charge VAT on the goods and the UK business will be able to reclaim the VAT on its next return	

Chapter 3 – Accounting for VAT

Task 3.1

Mr Green is a VAT-registered trader making standard-rated, zero-rated and exempt supplies.

Is he required to retain records of the amounts of different categories of supplies for VAT purposes?

TICK ONE BOX ON EACH LINE.

	Yes	No
Standard-rated supplies		
Zero-rated supplies		
Exempt supplies		

Task 3.2

A VAT-registered trader is required to keep adequate records to calculate the VAT due or reclaimable.

Complete the sentence below by inserting the appropriate number from the picklist.

VAT records should usually be retained for	▼	years.

Picklist:

1
2
6
20

Task 3.3

Mrs Violet is VAT-registered and runs a business making both cash and credit sales and purchases.

In order to calculate the correct amount of output tax for Mrs Violet's business, which of the following accounting records will be needed?

TICK ONE BOX ON EACH LINE.

	Yes	No
Sales day book		
Purchases day book		
Cash receipts book		
Cash payments book		

Task 3.4

Mrs Orange is VAT-registered and runs a business making both cash and credit sales and purchases.

In order to calculate the correct amount of input tax for Mrs Orange's business, which of the following accounting records will be needed?

TICK ONE BOX ON EACH LINE.

	Yes	No
Sales day book		
Purchases day book		
Cash receipts book		
Cash payments book		
Sales returns day book		
Purchases returns day book		

Task 3.5

Complete the sentence below by inserting the appropriate word from the picklist.

A trader must retain a valid VAT	▼	in order to reclaim input tax.

Picklist:

purchase order
invoice

....

Task 3.6

Identify which of the following details would not need to appear on a simplified or less detailed VAT invoice for a sale of no more than £250.00.

TICK ONE BOX.

	✓
The supplier's name and address	
The date of supply	
Description of the goods/services	
The total excluding VAT	

....

Task 3.7

Clipper Ltd holds the following invoices from suppliers.

(a)

VAT reg no 446 9989 57			Jupiter plc
Date: 4 January 20X0			1 London Road
Tax point: 4 January 20X0			Reading
Invoice no.			RL3 7CM
Clippers Ltd			
13 Gale Road			
Chester-le-Street			
NE1 1LB			

Sales of goods

Type	Quantity	VAT rate	Net
		%	£
Earrings @ £0.5 per unit	2,700	20	1,350.00
Earring studs @ £0.5 per unit	2,800	20	1,400.00
			2,750.00
VAT at 20%			550.00
Payable within 60 days			3,300.00

(b)

HILLSIDE LTD

'The Glasgow Based Supplier of Quality Jewellery Items'

VAT reg no 337 4849 26

Clipper Ltd

13 Gale Road

Chester-le-Street

NE1 1LB

Invoice no. 0010

Date: 10 August 20X0

Tax point: 10 August 20X0

	£
Sale of 4,000 Jewellery boxes @ £2 per unit	8,000
VAT at 20%	1,600
Total	9,600

Terms: strictly net 30 days

(c)

GENEROUS PLC

11 Low Fell
Leeds
LS1 XY2

Clipper Ltd
13 Gale Road
Chester-le-Street
NE1 1LB

Invoice no: 2221

Date: 12 December 20X0

Tax point: 12 December 20X0

	Net £	VAT £	Total £
4,000 Earrings @ £0.5 per unit	2,000.00	400.00	2,400.00
8,000 Brooches @ £0.3125 per unit	2,500.00	500.00	3,000.00
2,500 'How to make Jewellery' books @ £2 per book	5,000.00	0.00	5,000.00
	9,500.00	900.00	10,400.00

(d)

JEWELS & CO

101 High Street, Gateshead NE2 22P

VAT reg no 499 3493 27

Date: 2 February 20X0

30 necklaces sold for £4 each totalling £120.00 including VAT at 20%.

For each of the above invoices, state whether it is a valid VAT invoice. If it is not valid identify the missing item(s).

Choose from the following:

[Supplier's address, Invoice number, Supplier's VAT registration number, Applicable rates of VAT (0% & 20%)]

Invoice	Valid	Not valid	Missing item (s)	
(a)				▾
(b)				▾
(c)				▾
(d)				▾

Task 3.8

Identify which one of the following statements would need to appear on a pro forma invoice.

TICK ONE BOX.

	✓
This is a pro forma invoice	
This is not a VAT invoice	
This invoice does not allow input VAT recovery	
These goods have not yet been delivered	

Task 3.9

Mr Glass, a VAT-registered trader, has sent a credit note to a customer.

As a result of issuing this credit note, will Mr Glass have to pay more or less VAT to HMRC?

TICK ONE BOX.

More VAT payable	
Less VAT payable	

Task 3.10

Miss Spoon, a VAT-registered trader, has received a credit note from a supplier.

Which ONE of the following is the effect on VAT?

TICK ONE BOX.

	✓
Output tax will increase	
Output tax will decrease	
Input tax will increase	
Input tax will decrease	

Task 3.11

An invoice is dispatched to a customer on 13 August and the goods are delivered the following day.

What is the tax point in this situation and is it a basic tax point or an actual tax point?

TICK ONE BOX.

	✓
13 August and actual tax point	
13 August and basic tax point	
14 August and actual tax point	
14 August and basic tax point	

Task 3.12

A customer orders goods on 13 August. The goods are delivered on 15 August and the invoice is sent to the customer on 31 August. Payment for the goods is made on 15 September.

What is the tax point of this transaction?

TICK ONE BOX.

	✓
13 August	
15 August	
31 August	
15 September	

Task 3.13

Knife Ltd, a VAT-registered business, has not been paid by a customer for an invoice issued some time ago. The company now wishes to claim a refund of the VAT on that invoice from HMRC. It can do so provided certain conditions are fulfilled.

Which one of the following is NOT a relevant condition?

TICK ONE BOX.

	✓
Six months must have elapsed since payment was due	
Output tax has been accounted for and paid	
Notice must have been received from the customer's liquidators to state that it is insolvent	
The debt must have been written-off in the accounts of Knife Ltd	

Chapter 4 – The VAT return

Task 4.1

It is important for a VAT-registered trader to complete VAT returns regularly.

Complete the sentence below by inserting the appropriate number from the picklist.

VAT-registered traders must usually complete a VAT return every	▼	months.

Picklist:

3
6
9
36

Task 4.2

If input tax is greater than output tax in the VAT account, this will result in:

TICK ONE BOX.

	✓
a VAT payment due to HMRC	
a VAT repayment from HMRC	

Task 4.3

Cordelia's business has sales of approximately £200,000. She submits her VAT returns online and pays by BACS.

By what date should the VAT return to 31 May 20X0 be submitted?

TICK ONE BOX.

30 June 20X0	
7 July 20X0	
10 July 20X0	

By what date should any tax due for the return to 31 May 20X0 be paid?

TICK ONE BOX.

30 June 20X0	
7 July 20X0	
10 July 20X0	

Task 4.4

Charlotte's business has sales of approximately £200,000. She submits her VAT returns online and pays her VAT by direct debit.

By what date should the VAT return to 31 May 20X0 be submitted?

TICK ONE BOX.

30 June 20X0	
7 July 20X0	
10 July 20X0	

By what date would any tax due for the return to 31 May 20X0 be paid?

TICK ONE BOX.

30 June 20X0	
7 July 20X0	
10 July 20X0	

Task 4.5

(a) Happy Ltd is able to reclaim bad debt relief on an unpaid invoice.

   Which ONE of the following statements is correct? TICK ONE BOX.

	✓
Input tax reclaimable will be increased and the bad debt VAT will be included in box 4 on the VAT return.	
Output tax payable will be decreased and the bad debt VAT will be included as a deduction in box 1 on the VAT return.	

(b) Unhappy Ltd reclaims all the input tax on petrol provided to an employee for both business and private use, and will account for the private element of this by using the fuel scale charge.

Which ONE of the following statements is correct? TICK ONE BOX.

	✓
Output tax payable will be increased and the fuel scale charge will be included in box 1 on the VAT return.	
Input tax reclaimable will be decreased and the fuel scale charge will be included as a deduction in box 4 on the VAT return.	

Task 4.6

The following accounts have been extracted from the business ledgers.

Sales account

Date 20XX	Reference	Debit £	Date 20XX	Reference	Credit £
			1.10-31.12	Sales day book – UK sales	9,000.00
			1.10-31.12	Sales day book – EU despatches	3,550.00
31.12	Balance c/d	27,600.00	1.10-31.12	Cash book – UK sales	15,050.00
	Total	**27,600.00**		**Total**	**27,600.00**

Purchases and purchases returns account

Date 20XX	Reference	Debit £	Date 20XX	Reference	Credit £
1.10-31.12	Purchases day book – UK purchases	2,250.00	1.10-31.12	Purchases returns day book – UK purchases	975.00
1.10-31.12	Purchases day book – EU acquisitions	4,700.00	31.12	Balance c/d	5,975.00
	Total	**6,950.00**		**Total**	**6,950.00**

VAT account

Date 20XX	Reference	Debit £	Date 20XX	Reference	Credit £
1.10-31.12	Purchases day book	450.00	1.10-31.12	Sales day book	1,800.00
			1.10-31.12	Cash book – UK sales	3,010.00
			1.10-31.12	Purchases returns day book – UK purchases	195.00

The businesses EU acquisitions are goods that would normally be standard-rated.

EU despatches are to VAT-registered customers.

(a) **Complete the following:**

The figure for VAT due on EU acquisitions is:	£

(b) **Complete the following:**

The figure for box 1 of the VAT return is:	£

(c) **Complete the following:**

The figure for box 4 of the VAT return is:	£

Task 4.7

The following accounts have been extracted from a business's ledgers for quarter ended 31 May 20X1.

Sales and sales returns account

Date 20X1	Reference	Debit £	Date 20X1	Reference	Credit £
1.3-31.5	Sales returns day book – UK standard-rated sales	2,500.00	1.3-31.5	Sales day book – UK standard-rated sales	29,500.00
31.5	Balance c/d	44,000.00	1.3-31.5	Sales day book – UK zero-rated sales	17,000.00
	Total	46,500.00		Total	46,500.00

Purchases and purchases returns account

Date 20X1	Reference	Debit £	Date 20X1	Reference	Credit £
1.3-31.5	Purchases day book – UK standard-rated purchases	13,225.00	1.3-31.5	Purchases returns day book – UK standard-rated purchases	1,700.00
1.3-31.5	Purchases day book – EU purchases	2,140.00	31.5	Balance c/d	13,665.00
	Total	15,365.00		Total	15,365.00

VAT account

Date 20X1	Reference	Debit £	Date 20X1	Reference	Credit £
1.3-31.5	Sales returns day book	500.00	1.3-31.5	Sales day book	5,900.00
1.3-31.5	Purchases day book	2,645.00	1.3-31.5	Purchases returns day book	340.00

In May 20X1 a bad debt was written off as irrecoverable in the business's accounting records. The debt was for £720 (VAT-inclusive) on an invoice dated 27 October 20X0. Payment terms for the business are strictly 30 days from date of invoice.

The EU acquisitions are goods that would normally be standard-rated.

Complete boxes 1 to 9 of the VAT return below for quarter ended 31.5.20X1.

VAT return for quarter ended 31.5.20X1		£
VAT due in this period on **sales** and other outputs	Box 1	
VAT due in this period on **acquisitions** from other **EC Member States**	Box 2	
Total VAT due (**the sum of boxes 1 and 2**)	Box 3	
VAT reclaimed in this period on **purchases** and other inputs, including acquisitions from the EC	Box 4	
Net VAT to be paid to HM Revenue & Customs or reclaimed by you (**Difference between boxes 3 and 4 – if Box 4 is greater than Box 3, use a minus sign**)	Box 5	
Total value of **sales** and all other outputs excluding any VAT. **Include your box 8 figure. Whole pounds only**	Box 6	
Total value of **purchases** and all other inputs excluding any VAT. **Include your box 9 figure. Whole pounds only**	Box 7	
Total value of all **supplies** of goods and related costs, excluding any VAT, to other **EC Member States. Whole pounds only**	Box 8	
Total value of all **acquisitions** of goods and related costs, excluding any VAT, from other **EC Member States. Whole pounds only**	Box 9	

Chapter 5 – Schemes for small businesses

Task 5.1

Declan has heard that there is a special scheme available to some businesses that requires only one VAT return to be prepared each year.

Complete the sentences below by selecting/inserting the appropriate words/number.

Businesses submit only one return each year if they operate the	▼	scheme.

Picklist:

flat rate
annual accounting
cash accounting

To join, taxable supplies in the next 12 months must be below £	▼

Picklist:

150,000
230,000
1,350,000
1,600,000

Task 5.2

Complete the sentence below by selecting the appropriate words.

A business gets automatic bad debt relief if it operates the	▼	scheme.

Picklist:

flat rate
annual accounting
cash accounting

Task 5.3

Harry operates the flat rate scheme for his business.

Complete the sentence below by selecting the appropriate word.

Harry's VAT payable is calculated as a percentage of the VAT	▼	turnover.

Picklist:

inclusive
exclusive

Task 5.4

Debbie has a business with a year ended 30 April 20X0. Debbie operates the annual accounting scheme.

Which one of the following statements is correct?

TICK ONE BOX.

	✓
She pays some of her VAT by monthly instalments with the balance due by 31 May 20X0	
She pays some of her VAT by monthly instalments with the balance due by 30 June 20X0	
She pays all of her VAT in a single payment by 31 May 20X0	
She pays all of her VAT in a single payment by 30 June 20X0	

Task 5.5

Donald operates the cash accounting scheme.

Identify whether the following statements are True or False in relation to the cash accounting scheme.

	True	False
VAT is accounted for on the basis of cash paid and received rather than under the normal tax point rules		
The scheme is advantageous for businesses making only zero-rated supplies		
Businesses must leave the scheme if taxable supplies in the previous 12 months exceed £1,350,000		

Task 5.6

Jack operates the flat rate scheme.

Identify whether the following statements are True or False in relation to the flat rate scheme.

TICK ONE BOX ON EACH LINE.

	True	False
Businesses issue normal VAT invoices to customers		
VAT is paid in instalments		
The flat rate percentage applied depends on the type of business		
Less VAT may be payable by Jack as a result of operating the scheme		

Task 5.7

Would a business that gives its customers long periods of credit, but pays its suppliers promptly benefit from operating under the cash accounting scheme?

TICK ONE BOX.

	✓
Yes, because output VAT would be paid later and input VAT would be reclaimed at the same time or earlier	
No, because input VAT would be reclaimed later and output VAT would be paid at the same time or earlier	

Chapter 6 – Administration

Task 6.1

You have discovered an error on the VAT return of a client. You adjust for this error on the next VAT return if it is:

TICK ONE BOX.

	✓
More than the error correction reporting threshold, but not deliberate	
Less than the error correction reporting threshold and not deliberate	
More than the error correction reporting threshold and was deliberate	
Less than the error correction reporting threshold, but was deliberate	

Task 6.2

Amy's business has made a large error that exceeded the error correction reporting threshold, but was not careless or deliberate.

Identify whether the following statements are True or False in relation to this large error.

TICK ONE BOX.

	True	False
Amy can adjust this on her next return		
Amy cannot adjust this error on her next return and will be liable for a penalty		

Task 6.3

A business has made a small understatement of input tax in a previous quarter that is below the error correction threshold.

Should this adjustment be shown on the latest VAT return, and if so where on the return?

TICK ONE BOX.

	✓
No – not shown on the return	
Yes – shown in box 1	
Yes – shown in box 4	

Task 6.4

Adbul has just submitted his VAT return late. He has previously sent in all VAT returns on time.

For the purpose of your assessment, which one of the following statements is correct?

TICK ONE BOX.

	✓
No action will be taken by HMRC	
HMRC will issue a surcharge liability notice	
HMRC will issue a surcharge liability notice and charge a penalty	
HMRC charge a penalty only	

Task 6.5

Complete the sentence below by selecting the appropriate number.

A business has a requirement to retain VAT records for	▼	years.

Picklist:

three
four
six
ten

....

Task 6.6

Tax avoidance is illegal and consists of seeking to pay too little tax by deliberately misleading HMRC.

Decide whether this statement True or False.

TICK ONE BOX.

	✓
TRUE	
FALSE	

....

Task 6.7

Your client is Howard, who is currently VAT-registered. Howard's business is affected by a change in the VAT registration limits. Until now your client has had to be VAT-registered. However, the business has slowed down and the VAT registration/deregistration limits have increased. As a result your client could choose to deregister. Howard's customers are members of the general public and not VAT-registered.

Assume today's date is 1 June 20X0.

Draft an email to your client advising him of the options available to him.

To: [▼] (1)

From: [▼] (2)

Date: [▼] (3)

Subject: [▼] (4)

Please be advised that the current level of your business turnover is such that you are

able to VAT [▼] . (5) As you will no longer need to charge [▼] (6)

VAT to your customers, there are two options open to you.

1. Your selling prices can decrease to the VAT-exclusive amount

    As a result your profits will [▼] (7) At the same time your

    customers will have [▼] (8) cost.

2. Your selling prices can stay at the same VAT-inclusive amount

    As a result your profits will [▼] (9) At the same time your

    customers will have [▼] (10) cost.

If you wish to discuss this further please feel free to make an appointment.

Kind regards

Picklist:

(1)   Howard / AN Accountant
(2)   Howard / AN Accountant
(3)   1 June 20X0 / 31 March 20X0
(4)   VAT rates / VAT deregistration
(5)   register/ deregister
(6)   input / output
(7)   increase / decrease / stay the same.
(8)   the same / a higher / a lower
(9)   increase / decrease / stay the same.
(10)   the same / a higher / a lower

Task 6.8

It is 1 October 20X0 and you work for a firm of accountants, ABC & Co. Your client Mr Jones is considering joining the annual accounting scheme. Mr Jones' business operates from Unit 1 Alias Industrial Estate, Chelmsford, Essex, CM2 3FG.

You have been asked to complete the letter to Mr Jones explaining how the annual accounting scheme operates.

ABC & Co
2 Smith Street
London
W1 2DE

1 October 20X0

Mr Jones
Unit 1 Alias Industrial Estate
Chelmsford
Essex
CM2 3FG

Dear [▼] (1)

[▼] (2) **(subject)**

Further to our telephone conversation of today, I have set out below the details relating to the annual accounting scheme.

Your business can join the annual accounting scheme if the value of its taxable supplies [▼] (3) VAT, in the forthcoming [▼] (4) months does not exceed £ [▼] (5)

Under this scheme the business usually makes [▼] (6) equal monthly instalments. Each of these instalments is [▼] (7) of the prior year VAT liability.

173

The first payment is due at the [_____▼] (8) of the [_____▼] (9) month of the accounting period.

The balancing payment and the VAT return will be sent to HMRC within [_____▼] (10) of the end of the accounting period.

I hope that this has clarified the position. If you wish to discuss this further please do not hesitate to contact me.

Yours sincerely

Picklist:

(1)   Mr Jones / ABC & Co
(2)   Annual accounting scheme / Cash accounting scheme
(3)   including / excluding
(4)   3 / 12
(5)   150,000 / 1,350,000 / 1,600,000
(6)   four / nine / ten
(7)   ¼ / 1/10
(8)   beginning / end
(9)   first / third / fourth
(10)   30 days / a month and seven days / two months

Answer bank

Answer bank

Indirect Tax Answer Bank

Chapter 1

Task 1.1

Output tax	
Input tax	✓

....

Task 1.2

	✓
The retailer suffers a net cost of £5 VAT being the difference between its output and input tax on the product.	
The true cost of the product to the retailer is £120.	
The retailer does not bear any of the cost of VAT. The member of the public bears the full cost of £25 VAT.	✓
The retailer bears a VAT cost of £20 and the member of the public bears a VAT cost of £25.	

Provided the retailer makes only taxable supplies, it can recover its input VAT of £20 on its purchase and so suffers no VAT cost. The cost of the product to the retailer is therefore £100.

The retailer will collect £25 output VAT from the customer and pay it to HMRC but it suffers no VAT cost itself. The member of the public, the final consumer, suffers the full VAT of £25.

....

Task 1.3

	✓
The true cost of the product to the trader is £200.	
The trader suffers a VAT cost of £40.	✓
The trader accounts for output VAT of £40 on its purchase from the manufacturer.	
The member of the public suffers a VAT cost of £40.	

The trader is not VAT-registered. Therefore, it cannot recover input VAT of £40 on its purchase. The true cost of the product to the trader is therefore £240, the trader suffering the VAT of £40.

The trader does not account for VAT as it is not VAT-registered (and in any case this would be input VAT on the purchase, not output VAT).

The member of the public suffers no VAT, as the trader is not registered, so does not charge any VAT on the sale.

Task 1.4

	✓
Standard-rated supplies only	
Standard and zero-rated supplies	✓
Zero-rated and exempt supplies	
All three types of supply	

Task 1.5

Business	Yes, can reclaim ✓	No, cannot reclaim ✓
Bread Ltd – making only standard-rated supplies	✓	
Soup Ltd – making only exempt supplies		✓
Marmalade Ltd – making only zero-rated supplies	✓	

Task 1.6

Cost	✓
£0	
£20	
£100	✓
£120	

A VAT-registered trader making zero-rated supplies can recover all its input VAT and so the net cost of the goods is £100.

....

Task 1.7

	Correct ✓
Jam Ltd cannot register for VAT	
If Jam Ltd is VAT-registered it will make payments to HMRC	
If Jam Ltd is VAT-registered it will have repayments from HMRC	✓

Jam Ltd can recover input tax but has no output tax (charged at 0%), so will be in a net repayment position.

....

Task 1.8

	True	False
If Bradley's business makes zero-rated supplies, it will be in a VAT repayment position.	✓	
If Bradley makes standard-rated supplies, it could be disadvantageous for non VAT-registered customers.	✓	

If Bradley makes zero-rated supplies, he can recover his input tax but has no output tax (charged at 0%) so will be in a repayment position.

If Bradley makes standard-rated supplies, he will have to charge VAT at 20%. Non VAT-registered customers cannot recover this, and so the goods will be more expensive to them, unless Bradley decides to keep the price he charges to his customers the same.

....

Task 1.9

	Register now	Register within 30 days	Monitor and register later
An existing business with a total turnover of £6,650 per month for the last 12 months.			✓
A new business with an expected turnover of £25,000 per month for the next 12 months			✓
An existing business with a total turnover of £6,000 per month for the last 12 months. A new contract will bring in additional sales of £83,000 in 10 days time.	✓		

The first business has not exceeded the registration threshold of £82,000 in the last 12 months (£6,650 × 12 = £79,800) so does not have to register yet.

The new business has to register once it has exceeded the threshold in the last 12 months (or since starting to trade). It only has to register on the basis of its *expected* turnover if it is expected to exceed the threshold in the next 30 days *alone*. This is not the case.

The existing business has not exceeded the threshold in the last 12 months (£6,000 × 12 = £72,000). However the new contract means it will exceed the threshold in the next 30 days alone (£6,000 + £83,000 = £89,000), and so has to register now under the future test.

Task 1.10

	Can register	Cannot register
Blackberry Ltd – making only zero-rated supplies	✓	
Raspberry Ltd – making standard-rated and zero-rated supplies	✓	
Loganberry Ltd – making only exempt supplies		✓
Gooseberry Ltd – making standard-rated and exempt supplies .	✓	

Task 1.11

	True	False
Flan Ltd cannot register as it makes only zero-rated supplies		✓
Flan Ltd is automatically exempt from registering for VAT		✓
Flan Ltd can register for VAT	✓	
Flan Ltd can apply to HMRC to be exempt from registration	✓	

Flan Ltd is able to register for VAT, and must do so if it exceeds the registration threshold, but it is possible to apply to HMRC for exemption from registration as it makes only zero-rated supplies.

Task 1.12

	Include	Exclude
Standard-rated supplies	✓	
Zero-rated supplies	✓	
Exempt supplies		✓

Task 1.13

Taxable turnover in the next	**12**	months is expected to fall below the deregistration limit

Task 1.14

	✓
£80,000	✓
£82,000	
£150,000	
£1.35million	

Task 1.15

	True	False
The business can apply to HMRC for exception from registration, because the level of taxable supplies was temporary.	✓	

Chapter 2

Task 2.1

Invoice number	Net £	VAT £	Gross £
1000325	325.50	65.10	390.60
1000326	452.92	90.58	543.50

Workings:

£390.60 (gross) × 1/6 = £65.10 VAT, so net amount = £390.60 – £65.10 = £325.50

£452.92 (net) × 20% = £90.58 VAT, so gross amount = £452.92 + £90.58 = £543.50

....

Task 2.2

Circumstance	Yes, can reclaim	No, cannot reclaim
	✓	✓
Input tax incurred entertaining a UK client (meals provided during a meeting).		✓
Input tax incurred on the purchase of a van for use by a furniture repair business.	✓	
Input tax incurred providing meals on a training course for an employee.	✓	

....

Task 2.3

On the VAT return Dish Ltd must include an amount of account of the private fuel used by salesmen	**output**	tax to take

Output tax in the form of the fuel scale charge must be included.

....

Task 2.4

	✓
Nil	
£2,840.00	
£2,100.00	✓
£4,940.00	

VAT is irrecoverable on cars purchased where there is both business and private use.

Task 2.5

	✓
All input tax can be reclaimed	
Only input tax relating to standard rated supplies can be reclaimed	
All input tax can be reclaimed provided certain de minimis tests are met	✓
Only input tax relating to standard and zero-rated supplies can be reclaimed	
No input tax can be reclaimed	

Task 2.6

This purchase is known as an	**acquisition.**

Task 2.7

In order to benefit from zero rating the customer must provide	**his EU VAT-registration number**

Task 2.8

Goods exported to customers outside the EU must be treated as	**zero-rated**

Task 2.9

	Correct
VAT payable to HMRC of £3,100	
VAT reclaimed from HMRC of £3,100	
Nil net VAT effect	✓

VAT is paid to HMRC at the airport/port and then reclaimed as input tax on the VAT return, so the net effect is the same as a purchase in the UK, ie nil net VAT effect.

••

Task 2.10

	✓
As long as the UK business supplies its VAT number to the EU supplier the goods will be zero-rated and VAT doesn't need to be accounted for	
The UK business will charge itself output tax for the goods on its VAT return and reclaim input tax on the same return	✓
The UK business will pay output tax to HMRC at the point of entry into the UK and reclaim input tax on the next return	
The EU supplier will charge VAT on the goods and the UK business will be able to reclaim the VAT on its next return	

The first statement is incorrect as the UK business must account for output tax and reclaim input tax (although the EU supplier would treat the supply as zero-rated).

The third statement is incorrect as this describes the position for an import from outside the EU.

The fourth statement is incorrect as it is the UK business (and not the EU supplier) which must account for the output tax.

••

Chapter 3

Task 3.1

	Yes	No
Standard-rated supplies	✓	
Zero-rated supplies	✓	
Exempt supplies	✓	

Task 3.2

VAT records should usually be retained for	6	years.

Task 3.3

	Yes	No
Sales day book	✓	
Purchases day book		✓
Cash receipts book	✓	
Cash payments book		✓

Task 3.4

	Yes	No
Sales day book		✓
Purchases day book	✓	
Cash receipts book		✓
Cash payments book	✓	
Sales returns day book		✓
Purchases returns day book	✓	

Task 3.5

A trader must retain a valid VAT	**invoice**	in order to reclaim input tax.

....

Task 3.6

	✓
The supplier's name and address	
The date of supply	
Description of the goods/ services	
The total excluding VAT	✓

For each applicable VAT rate the total including VAT is required together with the rates.

....

Task 3.7

Invoice	Valid	Not valid	Missing item (s)
(a)		✓	Invoice number
(b)		✓	Supplier's address
(c)		✓	Supplier's VAT registration number/ Applicable rates of VAT(0% & 20%)
(d)	✓		

Note:

The total value of the supply by Jewels & Co (d), including VAT, does not exceed £250, so a less detailed invoice is permissible.

The invoice is valid, because it includes all the information which must be shown on a less detailed invoice.

....

Task 3.8

	✓
This is a pro forma invoice	
This is not a VAT invoice	✓
This invoice does not allow input VAT recovery	
These goods have not yet been delivered	

Task 3.9

More VAT payable	
Less VAT payable	✓

The credit note will decrease the output tax, and so less VAT will be payable.

Task 3.10

	✓
Output tax will increase	
Output tax will decrease	
Input tax will increase	
Input tax will decrease	✓

Task 3.11

	✓
13 August and actual tax point	✓
13 August and basic tax point	
14 August and actual tax point	
14 August and basic tax point	

The basic tax point is 14 August, the date of delivery of the goods, but the invoice date is before this so the tax point is an actual tax point of 13 August.

Task 3.12

	✓
13 August	
15 August	✓
31 August	
15 September	

The basic tax point is 15 August, the date of delivery of the goods, and the invoice is issued more than 14 days later so this does not create an actual tax point.

....

Task 3.13

	✓
Six months must have elapsed since payment was due	
Output tax has been accounted for and paid	
Notice must have been received from the customer's liquidators to state that it is insolvent	✓
The debt must have been written-off in the accounts of Knife Ltd	

....

Chapter 4

Task 4.1

VAT-registered traders must usually complete a VAT return every	3	months.

Task 4.2

	✓
a VAT payment due to HMRC	
a VAT repayment from HMRC	✓

Task 4.3

VAT return to 31 May 20X0 submission date

30 June 20X0	
7 July 20X0	✓
10 July 20X0	

VAT due

30 June 20X0	
7 July 20X0	✓
10 July 20X0	

Task 4.4

VAT return to 31 May 20X0 submission date

30 June 20X0	
7 July 20X0	✓
10 July 20X0	

VAT due

30 June 20X0	
7 July 20X0	
10 July 20X0	✓

Task 4.5

(a)

	✓
Input tax reclaimable will be increased and the bad debt VAT will be included in box 4 on the VAT return	✓
Output tax payable will be decreased and the bad debt VAT will be included as a deduction in box 1 on the VAT return	

(b)

	✓
Output tax payable will be increased and the fuel scale charge will be included in box 1 on the VAT return	✓
Input tax reclaimable will be decreased and the fuel scale charge will be included as a deduction in box 4 on the VAT return	

Task 4.6

(a)

The figure for VAT due on EU acquisitions is:	£ 940.00

(b)

The figure for box 1 of the VAT return is:	£ 4,810.00

VAT due in this period on sales and other outputs = £1,800 + £3,010

(c)

The figure for box 4 of the VAT return is:	£ 1,195.00

VAT reclaimed in the period on purchases and other inputs, including acquisitions from the EU = £450 – £195 + £940

Task 4.7

VAT return for quarter ended 31.5.20X1		£
VAT due in this period on **sales** and other outputs	Box 1	5,400.00
VAT due in this period on **acquisitions** from other **EC Member States**	Box 2	428.00
Total VAT due (**the sum of boxes 1 and 2**)	Box 3	5,828.00
VAT reclaimed in this period on **purchases** and other inputs, including acquisitions from the EC	Box 4	2,853.00
Net VAT to be paid to HM Revenue & Customs or reclaimed by you (**Difference between boxes 3 and 4 – if Box 4 is greater than Box 3, use a minus sign**)	Box 5	2,975.00
Total value of **sales** and all other outputs excluding any VAT. **Include your box 8 figure. Whole pounds only**	Box 6	44,000
Total value of **purchases** and all other inputs excluding any VAT. **Include your box 9 figure. Whole pounds only**	Box 7	13,665
Total value of all **supplies** of goods and related costs, excluding any VAT, to other **EC Member States. Whole pounds only**	Box 8	0
Total value of all **acquisitions** of goods and related costs, excluding any VAT, from other **EC Member States. Whole pounds only**	Box 9	2,140

		£
Workings:		
Box 1	VAT on sales from the sales day book	5,900.00
	Less: VAT on credit notes	(500.00)
		5,400.00
Box 2	VAT due on EU acquisitions (2,140 × 20%)	**428.00**
Box 3	Total of box 1 and box 2 £5,400 + £428	**5,828.00**
Box 4	VAT on purchases from purchases day book	2,645.00
	VAT on EU acquisitions	428.00
	Bad debt relief (720.00 × 1/6)	120.00
	Less: VAT on credit notes	(340.00)
		2,853.00
Box 5	Net VAT due Box 3 minus box 4 £5,828 – £2,853	**2,975.00**
Box 6	Zero-rated credit UK sales	17,000.00
	Standard-rated credit UK sales	29,500.00
	Less: standard-rated credit notes	(2,500.00)
		44,000
Box 7	Standard-rated credit UK purchases	13,225.00
	EU purchases	2,140.00
	Less: standard-rated credit notes	(1,700.00)
		13,665
Box 8	EU sales	**0**
Box 9	EU acquisitions	**2,140**

Chapter 5

Task 5.1

Businesses submit only one return each year if they operate the	**annual accounting**	scheme

To join, taxable supplies in the next 12 months must be below £	**1,350,000**

Task 5.2

A business gets automatic bad debt relief if it operates the	**cash accounting**	scheme

Task 5.3

Harry's VAT payable is calculated as a percentage of the VAT	**inclusive**	turnover

Task 5.4

	✓
She pays some of her VAT by monthly instalments with the balance due by 31 May 20X0	
She pays some of her VAT by monthly instalments with the balance due by 30 June 20X0	✓
She pays all of her VAT in a single payment by 31 May 20X0	
She pays all of her VAT in a single payment by 30 June 20X0	

Task 5.5

	True	False
VAT is accounted for on the basis of cash paid and received rather than under the normal tax point rules	✓	
The scheme is advantageous for businesses making only zero-rated supplies		✓*
Businesses must leave the scheme if taxable supplies in the previous 12 months exceed £1,350,000		✓**

*   Input tax is generally reclaimed later under the cash accounting scheme, so this is not advantageous

**   The limit for leaving is £1,600,000

Task 5.6

	True	False
Businesses issue normal VAT invoices to customers	✓	
VAT is paid in instalments		✓
The flat rate percentage applied depends on the type of business	✓	
Less VAT may be payable by Jack as a result of operating the scheme	✓	

Task 5.7

	✓
Yes, because output VAT would be paid later and input VAT would be reclaimed at the same time or earlier	✓
No, because input VAT would be reclaimed later and output VAT would be paid at the same time or earlier	

Chapter 6

Task 6.1

	✓
More than the error correction reporting threshold, but not deliberate	
Less than the error correction reporting threshold and not deliberate	✓
More than the error correction reporting threshold and was deliberate	
Less than the error correction reporting threshold, but was deliberate	

Task 6.2

	True	False
Amy can adjust this on her next return		✓
Amy cannot adjust this error on her next return and will be liable for a penalty		✓

Amy cannot adjust this error on her next return but there will not be a penalty as it was not careless or deliberate.

Task 6.3

	✓
No – not shown on the return	
Yes – shown in box 1	
Yes – shown in box 4	✓

It is shown as an increase in the input tax at box 4 on the VAT return.

Task 6.4

No action will be taken by HMRC	
HMRC will issue a surcharge liability notice	✓
HMRC will issue a surcharge liability notice and charge a penalty	
HMRC charge a penalty only	

Task 6.5

A business has a requirement to retain VAT records for	**six**	years.

Task 6.6

TRUE	
FALSE	✓

Tax avoidance is a way of trying to legally reduce your tax burden, whereas tax evasion is illegal and consists of seeking to pay too little tax by deliberately misleading HMRC.

Task 6.7

To: **Howard**
From: **AN Accountant**
Date: **1 June 20X0**
Subject: **VAT deregistration**

Please be advised that the current level of your business turnover is such that you are able to VAT **deregister**. As you will no longer need to charge **output** VAT to your customers, there are two options open to you.

(1) Your selling prices can decrease to the VAT-exclusive amount. As a result your profits will **stay the same**. At the same time your customers will have **a lower** cost.

(2) Your selling prices can stay at the same VAT-inclusive amount. As a result your profits will **increase**. At the same time your customers will have **the same** cost.

If you wish to discuss this further please feel free to make an appointment.

Kind regards

Task 6.8

ABC & Co
2 Smith Street
London
W1 2DE

1 October 20X0

Mr Jones
Unit 1 Alias Industrial Estate
Chelmsford
Essex
CM2 3FG

Dear Mr Jones

Annual accounting scheme

Further to our telephone conversation of today, I have set out below the details relating to the annual accounting scheme.

Your business can join the annual accounting scheme if the value of its taxable supplies **excluding** VAT, in the forthcoming **12** months does not exceed **£1,350,000.**

Under this scheme the business usually makes **nine** equal monthly instalments. Each of these instalments is **1/10** of the prior year VAT liability. The first payment is due at the **end** of the **fourth** month of the accounting period.

The balancing payment and the VAT return will be sent to HMRC within **two months** of the end of the accounting period.

I hope that this has clarified the position. If you wish to discuss this further please do not hesitate to contact me.

Yours sincerely

Answer bank

AAT AQ2013 SAMPLE ASSESSMENT 1 INDIRECT TAX (ITAX)

AAT AQ2013 SAMPLE ASSESSMENT 1

Task 1 (5 marks)

A VAT-registered business makes both standard rated and zero-rated supplies. It has been registered for many years. The business had sales of £8,000 per month in the year ended 31 December 20X1. From 1 January 20X2 sales will decrease and it is estimated monthly turnover will be £4,000 per month.

(a) **Which ONE of the following statements most accurately describes the business's VAT registration requirement on 30 June 20X2?**

Because the business has been registered for many years it must remain registered. ☐

The business must deregister as its taxable turnover will have dropped below the VAT registration threshold. ☐

The business will have dropped below the VAT deregistration threshold so may deregister if it wishes. ☐

A VAT-registered trader is seeking advice on keeping VAT records for VAT inspections.

(b) **Complete the following statements by choosing ONE option in each case.**

His immediate action should be to [▼]

If this fails to produce the advice he should [▼]

If the query remains unresolved he should [▼]

Picklist:

consult the HMRC website
write to HMRC
telephone the VAT helpline

Task 2 (7 marks)

A VAT-registered business sells a variety of standard-rated and zero-rated items and wishes to use the simplified invoice rules.

(a) **Which ONE of the following statements is TRUE?**

The business may issue a simplified invoice for a mixed supply of standard-rated items of £200 gross and zero-rated items of £45.	☐
The business may issue a simplified invoice for standard-rated items of £245 plus VAT.	☐
The business may issue a simplified invoice for a mixed supply of zero-rated items of £200 and standard-rated items of £45 plus VAT.	☐

(b) **Which ONE of the following items of information can be omitted from a simplified invoice?**

The tax point	☐
The amount of VAT	☐
The seller's VAT registration number	☐
The seller's address	☐

A VAT-registered business makes supplies of both standard-rated and exempt items. The amount of input tax incurred relating to its exempt supplies is above the minimum de minimis amount.

(c) **Which ONE of the following statements is TRUE?**

All its input tax can be reclaimed because the de minimis amount is exceeded.	☐
None of its input tax can be reclaimed because the de minimis amount is exceeded.	☐
Some of its input tax can be reclaimed, in proportion to the different types of supply.	☐

Task 3 (5 marks)

A VAT-registered business operates a single special accounting scheme for VAT and has the following characteristics:

- It joined the scheme when its taxable turnover was less than £1.35m per year.
- Its taxable turnover remains less than £1.6m per year.
- It only pays output tax to HMRC when it has been received from its customers.
- It only reclaims input tax from HMRC when it has been paid to its suppliers.

(a) **Which ONE of the following schemes is being used?**

The annual accounting scheme ☐

The cash accounting scheme ☐

The flat rate scheme ☐

A registered business is using the flat rate scheme.

(b) **Can the business use one of the other special accounting schemes with the flat rate scheme?**

Yes, it can use the annual accounting scheme ☐

Yes, it can use the cash accounting scheme ☐

No, it cannot use any other special accounting scheme ☐

(c) **Complete the following statement in respect of the availability of bad debt relief to a VAT-registered trader.**

Bad debt relief is available when a debt has been written off and is [▾].

Picklist:

at least six months overdue
more than four and a half years old

....

Task 4 (7 marks)

(a) **Complete the following statements by choosing ONE option in each case.**

A VAT-registered business in the UK which sells goods to a business in a country outside the EU is making [▼] .

Picklist:

an acquisition
a despatch
an export
an import

A supply is normally zero-rated if it is to a business [▼] .

Picklist:

that is not VAT registered but is within the EU
that is outside the EU

A business has received a surcharge liability notice from HMRC.

(b) **Complete the following statements choosing ONE option in each case.**

The notice would only have been issued if the business

[▼] .

Picklist:

had missed the due date for submitting its VAT return
had failed to register for VAT at the correct time

The notice [▼] .

Picklist:

imposes an immediate surcharge

puts the business in a surcharge period for 12 months

requires the business to pay over all outstanding output tax immediately as a surcharge

Task 5 (6 marks)

A VAT-registered business trades in camping equipment. It makes a mixed supply to a customer as follows:

- Standard-rated items for £683.94 plus VAT
- Zero-rated items for £128

(a) **How much VAT should be included on the VAT invoice? Choose ONE option.**

£25.60 ☐

£136.78 ☐

£136.79 ☐

£162.38 ☐

The business makes a further supply to the customer as follows:

- Standard-rated items for £1,287.60, including VAT
- Exempt items for £142.92

(b) **How much should the trader include as output tax on its VAT return in respect of this sale? Choose ONE option.**

£23.82 ☐

£214.60 ☐

£257.52 ☐

£286.10 ☐

Task 6 (6 marks)

This task is about preparing figures for a business's VAT Return for the period ended 30 June.

The standard rate of VAT is 20%.

The following accounts have been extracted from the ledgers:

Purchases account

Date	Reference	Debit £	Date	Reference	Credit £
01.04-30.06	Purchases day book – UK purchases	455,328.54			
01.04-30.06	Purchases day book – zero-rated imports	39,824.73	30.06	Balance c/d	495,153.27
	Total	495,153.27		Total	495,153.27

VAT account

Date	Reference	Debit £	Date	Reference	Credit £
01.04-30.06	Purchases day book – UK purchases	91,065.70	01.04-30.06	Sales day book – UK sales	193,582.01
			01.04-30.06	Cash book – UK sales	3,281.68

You are told that UK purchases included a company car for £35,834 plus VAT. The related VAT for the purchase is included in the VAT account figure. Because it cannot be reclaimed, the VAT should be included in the purchases account.

(a) **Calculate the figure for Box 1 of the VAT return – VAT due in this period on sales and other outputs.**

£ [ ]

(b) **Calculate the figure for Box 4 of the VAT return – VAT reclaimed on purchases and other inputs.**

£ [ ]

(c) **Calculate the figure for Box 7 of the VAT return – value of purchases and all other inputs, excluding any VAT. Whole pounds only.**

£ [ ]

Task 7 (17 marks)

This task is about preparing all the figures for completion of a business's online VAT return for the period ended 31 October.

The following accounts have been extracted from the ledgers:

Sales account

Date	Reference	Debit £	Date	Reference	Credit £
			01.08-31.10	Sales day book – UK sales	365,005.32
31.10	Balance c/d	374,192.93	01.08-31.10	Sales day book – EU despatches	9,187.61
	Total	374,192.93		Total	374,192.93

Purchases account

Date	Reference	Debit £	Date	Reference	Credit £
01.08-31.10	Purchases day book – UK purchases	109,997.26			
01.08-31.10	Purchases day book – zero-rated imports	2,586.92	31.10	Balance c/d	112,584.18
	Total	112,584.18		Total	112,584.18

VAT account

Date	Reference	Debit £	Date	Reference	Credit £
01.08-31.10	Purchases day book – UK purchases	21,999.45	01.08-31.10	Sales day book – UK sales	73,001.06

You are told that output tax in relation to a standard-rated net sale of £1,462.20 was omitted from the Box 1 figure on the previous period's VAT Return. This is to be adjusted in Box 1 of this VAT Return. No other adjustments are to be made.

Enter the figures for boxes 1 to 9 of the online VAT return for the period ended 31 October. Do not leave any box blank.

Online VAT return for period ended 31 October		£
VAT due in this period on sales and other outputs (Box 1)	for Box 1	
VAT due in this period on acquisitions from other EC member states (Box 2)	for Box 2	
Total VAT due (the sum of boxes 1 and 2) (Box 3)	for Box 3	
VAT reclaimed in this period on purchases and other inputs, including acquisitions from the EC (Box 4)	for Box 4	
Net VAT to be paid to HM Revenue & Customs or reclaimed by you (Difference between boxes 3 and 4 – if Box 4 is greater than Box 3, use a minus sign) (for Box 5)	for Box 5	
Total value of sales and all other outputs excluding any VAT. Include your box 8 figure (Box 6). Whole pounds only	for Box 6	
Total value of purchases and all other inputs excluding any VAT. Include your box 9 figure (Box 7). Whole pounds only	for Box 7	
Total value of all supplies of goods and related costs, excluding any VAT, to other EC member states (Box 8). Whole pounds only.	for Box 8	
Total value of all acquisitions of goods and related costs, excluding any VAT, from other EC member states (Box 9). Whole pounds only	for Box 9	

Task 8 (7 marks)

You are an accounting technician for a retail business, reporting to the chief accountant. You have been asked to report on how an increase in the rate of VAT would affect the business and what action would have to be taken as a consequence.

Today's date is 28 May.

Prepare a draft email to the chief accountant providing information about some of the potential effects and consequences of a change. Choose ONE option to complete each sentence.

To:	[▼]
From:	[▼]
Date:	28 May
Subject:	Change of VAT rate

When the rate of VAT changes the business must consider what prices it will charge to customers. These prices [▼].

The new rate of VAT must be reflected in the amount of VAT paid to HMRC
[▼].

If the date of the VAT change falls during a VAT period, our system must
[▼].

Kind regards

Accounting Technician

Picklists:

Accounting Technician / Chief accountant

Accounting Technician / Chief accountant

cannot change until the date of the next VAT return / must change on the date of the VAT change as specified by HMRC / can remain unchanged if the business desires

only if the business chooses to change its prices to customers / whether the business changes its prices to customers or not / only if customers choose to pay the new prices

apply a single rate of VAT during that VAT period / apply dual rates of VAT during that VAT period depending on the customer / apply dual rates of VAT during that VAT period depending on each transaction's tax point

....

AAT SAMPLE ASSESSMENT 1
INDIRECT TAX (ITAX – AQ2013)

ANSWERS

Task 1 (5 marks)

(a) **Which ONE of the following statements most accurately describes the business's VAT registration requirement on 30 June 20X2?**

Because the business has been registered for many years it must remain registered. ☐

The business must deregister as its taxable turnover will have dropped below the VAT registration threshold. ☐

The business will have dropped below the VAT deregistration threshold so may deregister if it wishes. ☑

A VAT-registered trader is seeking advice on keeping VAT records for VAT inspections.

(b) **Complete the following statements by choosing ONE option in each case.**

His immediate action should be to | consult the HMRC website ▼ |

If this fails to produce the advice he should | telephone the VAT helpline ▼ |

If the query remains unresolved he should | write to HMRC ▼ |

···

Task 2 (7 marks)

(a) **Which ONE of the following statements is TRUE?**

The business may issue a simplified invoice for a mixed supply of standard-rated items of £200 gross and zero-rated items of £45. ☑

The business may issue a simplified invoice for standard-rated items of £245 plus VAT. ☐

The business may issue a simplified invoice for a mixed supply of zero-rated items of £200 and standard-rated items of £45 plus VAT. ☐

(b) **Which ONE of the following items of information can be omitted from a simplified invoice?**

The tax point ☐

The amount of VAT ☑

The seller's VAT registration number ☐

The seller's address ☐

BPP
LEARNING MEDIA

A VAT-registered business makes supplies of both standard-rated and exempt items. The amount of input tax incurred relating to its exempt supplies is above the minimum de minimis amount.

(c) **Which ONE of the following statements is TRUE?**

All its input tax can be reclaimed because the de minimis amount is exceeded. ☐

None of its input tax can be reclaimed because the de minimis amount is exceeded. ☐

Some of its input tax can be reclaimed, in proportion to the different types of supply. ☑

Task 3 (5 marks)

(a) **Which ONE of the following schemes is being used?**

The annual accounting scheme ☐

The cash accounting scheme ☑

The flat rate scheme ☐

(b) **Can the business use one of the other special accounting schemes with the flat rate scheme?**

Yes, it can use the annual accounting scheme ☑

Yes, it can use the cash accounting scheme ☐

No, it cannot use any other special accounting scheme ☐

(c) **Complete the following statement in respect of the availability of bad debt relief to a VAT-registered trader.**

Bad debt relief is available when a debt has been written off and is
| at least six months overdue ▼ | .

Task 4 (7 marks)

(a) **Complete the following statements by choosing ONE option in each case.**

A VAT-registered business in the UK which sells goods to a business in a country outside the EU is making | an export ▼ |.

A supply is normally zero-rated if it is to a business | that is outside the EU ▼ |.

A business has received a surcharge liability notice from HMRC.

(b) **Complete the following statements choosing ONE option in each case.**

The notice would only have been issued if the business

| had missed the due date for submitting its VAT return. ▼ |

The notice | puts the business in a surcharge period for 12 months ▼ |.

Task 5 (6 marks)

(a) **How much VAT should be included on the VAT invoice? Choose ONE option.**

£25.60 ☐

£136.78 ☑

£136.79 ☐

£162.38 ☐

(b) **How much should the trader include as output tax on its VAT return in respect of this sale? Choose ONE option.**

£23.82 ☐

£214.60 ☑

£257.52 ☐

£286.10 ☐

Task 6 (6 marks)

(a) **Calculate the figure for Box 1 of the VAT return – VAT due in this period on sales and other outputs.**

£	196,863.69

Working: £193,582.01 + £3,281.68 = £196,863.69

(b) **Calculate the figure for Box 4 of the VAT return – VAT reclaimed on purchases and other inputs.**

£	83,898.90

The VAT on the company car is not recoverable because of the private useage.

Working: £91,065.70 – (£35,834 × 20%) = £83,898.90

(c) **Calculate the figure for Box 7 of the VAT return – value of purchases and all other inputs, excluding any VAT. Whole pounds only.**

£	502,320

Or

£	502,319

Or

£	495,153.27

Working: £495,153.27 + (£35,834 × 20%) = £502,320

Or £495,153.27 – AAT have confirmed that the instructions to this question were not clear enough, therefore they will accept either the figure including or excluding the irrecoverable VAT on the company car in box 7.

Task 7 (17 marks)

Enter the figures for boxes 1 to 9 of the online VAT return for the period ended 31 October. Do not leave any box blank.

Online VAT return for period ended 31 October		£
VAT due in this period on sales and other outputs (Box 1)	for Box 1	73,293.50
VAT due in this period on acquisitions from other EC member states (Box 2)	for Box 2	0.00
Total VAT due (the sum of boxes 1 and 2) (Box 3)	for Box 3	73,293.50
VAT reclaimed in this period on purchases and other inputs, including acquisitions from the EC (Box 4)	for Box 4	21,999.45
Net VAT to be paid to HM Revenue & Customs or reclaimed by you (Difference between boxes 3 and 4 – if Box 4 is greater than Box 3, use a minus sign) (for Box 5)	for Box 5	51,294.05
Total value of sales and all other outputs excluding any VAT. Include your box 8 figure (Box 6). Whole pounds only	for Box 6	374,192 Or 374,1923
Total value of purchases and all other inputs excluding any VAT. Include your box 9 figure (Box 7). Whole pounds only	for Box 7	112,584 Or 112,585
Total value of all supplies of goods and related costs, excluding any VAT, to other EC member states (Box 8). Whole pounds only	for Box 8	9,187 Or 9,188
Total value of all acquisitions of goods and related costs, excluding any VAT, from other EC member states (Box 9). Whole pounds only	for Box 9	0

Rounding – Boxes 6 to 8

This model answer shows the figures in **boxes 6 to 8** rounded down, however figures rounded up are equally valid for the purposes of this assessment.

Task 8 (7 marks)

Prepare a draft email to the chief accountant providing information about some of the potential effects and consequences of a change. Choose ONE option to complete each sentence.

To: Chief accountant ▼

From: Accounting Technician ▼

Date: 28 May

Subject: Change of VAT rate

When the rate of VAT changes the business must consider what prices it will charge to customers. These prices | can remain unchanged if the business desires ▼ .

The new rate of VAT must be reflected in the amount of VAT paid to HMRC | whether the business changes its prices to customers or not ▼ .

If the date of the VAT change falls during a VAT period, our system must | apply dual rates of VAT during that VAT period depending on each transaction's tax point ▼ .

Kind regards

Accounting Technician

BPP PRACTICE ASSESSMENT 1
INDIRECT TAX (ITAX – AQ2013)

Time allowed: 1.5 hours

Indirect Tax Practice Assessment 1

Task 1

(a) Joseph makes zero-rated supplies and Julie makes standard-rated supplies. Both are considering voluntarily registering for VAT. Julie's customers are mostly VAT-registered themselves.

Identify whether the following statements are True or False.

TICK ONE BOX per statement.

	True	False
Joseph will be in a repayment position if he voluntarily registers		
Julie's customers will not suffer the impact of her charging VAT unless they are not VAT-registered		

(b) Clover Ltd has been trading for 12 months. You have extracted the following information in relation to the company.

Turnover	VAT excl £
Standard-rated	61,000
Zero-rated	13,000
Exempt	8,000

Identify whether the following statement is True or False. TICK ONE BOX.

	True	False
Assuming Clover Ltd was not VAT-registered from starting to trade		
Clover Ltd must VAT register as total turnover exceeds £82,000		

....

Task 2

Adam is a VAT-registered trader making standard-rated supplies. On 19 March 20X0 he received an order from a customer together with a 10% deposit including VAT of £40. The goods were sent out to the customer on 22 March 20X0. An invoice was sent out on 1 April 20X0 that included VAT of £400. The customer paid the balance of the invoice (including VAT of £360) on 30 April 20X0.

Calculate the amount of output tax to be included on Adam's VAT return to:

(a) **31 March 20X0**

TICK ONE BOX.

	✓
Nil	
£40	
£360	
£400	

(b) **30 June 20X0**

TICK ONE BOX.

	✓
Nil	
£40	
£360	
£400	

(c) A VAT-registered business makes a mixture of exempt and taxable supplies.

Which of the following statements is true?

TICK ONE BOX.

	✓
Only the input tax relating to taxable supplies is recoverable, in all circumstances	
All input tax is recoverable if certain de minimis tests are satisfied	
No input tax is recoverable	
All input tax is recoverable as no supplies are outside the scope of VAT	

Task 3

Igor has been trading for many years and makes standard-rated supplies. He is in the flat rate scheme. The flat rate percentage that he must use is 10.5%.

In the latest quarter, Igor had total turnover of £9,000 excluding VAT. He also had VAT-exclusive purchases of £2,000.

(a) **Identify which one of the following is the output tax figure to be included in Igor's VAT return.**

TICK ONE BOX.

	✓
£945.00	
£1,134.00	
£882.00	

(b) **In this quarter, would Igor have more or less VAT to pay to HMRC if he was not in the flat rate scheme?**

TICK ONE BOX.

	✓
More VAT payable if not in the flat rate scheme	
Less VAT payable if not in the flat rate scheme	

(c) **Which one of the following is not a valid reason for a business making taxable supplies choosing to operate the annual accounting scheme?**

TICK ONE BOX.

	✓
Only one VAT return per annum is required	
It helps regulate cash flow	
It reduces the administrative burden on the business	
Only one VAT payment per annum is required	

Task 4

(a) **You have extracted the following information from the accounting records of a client.**

Detail	Net £	VAT £	Gross £
Car (for use by salesman)	14,000.00	2,800.00	16,800.00
Hotels (for sales reps while on business)	2,400.00	480.00	2,880.00
UK client lunches	460.00	92.00	552.00

Calculate the total amount of input tax that is recoverable by the client relating to these items of expenditure.

TICK ONE BOX.

	✓
Nil	
£92.00	
£480.00	
£3,372.00	

(b) **Identify whether the following statements are True or False.**

TICK ONE BOX PER STATEMENT.

	True	False
If a trader submits an inaccurate VAT return but tells HMRC of the inaccuracy as soon as possible, this may reduce the possible penalty		
Tax evasion is illegal and may lead to fines and imprisonment		

Task 5

(a) A VAT-registered trader makes a mixed supply to a customer as follows:

- Standard rated items for £133.18 including VAT
- Zero rated items for £821.99

What is the amount of the VAT on the invoice?

The amount of VAT on the invoice is	£	

(b) The correct VAT payable by a business for the quarter ended 31 December 20X1 is shown on the VAT return as £18,400.00. However, the VAT account at the end of this period shows a balance of £28,400.00.

Which of the following statements could explain the difference?

TICK ONE BOX.

	✓
The VAT payment for the previous period of £5,000.00 was not posted to the VAT account	
The VAT payment for the previous period of £5,000.00 was posted to the wrong side of the VAT account	

Task 6

The following accounts have been extracted from Company A's ledgers for quarter ended 31 December 20X0.

Sales account

Date 20X0	Reference	Debit £	Date 20X0	Reference	Credit £
			1.9-31.12	Sales day book – UK standard-rated sales	70,000.00
31.12	Balance c/d	85,000.00	1.9-31.12	Sales day book – UK zero-rated sales	15,000.00
	Total	85,000.00		Total	85,000.00

Purchases and purchases returns account

Date 20X0	Reference	Debit £	Date 20X0	Reference	Credit £
1.9-31.12	Purchases day book – UK standard-rated purchases	17,200.00	1.9-31.12	Purchases returns day book – UK standard-rated purchases	2,300.00
1.9-31.12	Purchases day book – UK zero-rated purchases	2,500.00	31.12	Balance c/d	17,400.00
	Total	19,700.00		Total	19,700.00

VAT account

Date 20X0	Reference	Debit £	Date 20X0	Reference	Credit £
1.9-31.12	Purchases day book	3,440.00	1.9-31.12	Sales day book	14,000.00
			1.9-31.12	Purchases returns day book	460.00

In December 20X0 two debts (on standard-rated sales) were written off as irrecoverable (bad) in Company A's accounting records. The first debt was for £758 on an invoice dated 15 March 20X0; the second was for £622 with an invoice dated 23 June 20X0. Company A's payment terms are strictly 30 days from date of invoice. Both figures are stated inclusive of VAT.

(a) **Calculate the figure to be reclaimed for bad debt relief in the quarter ended 31.12.20X0.**

The figure to be reclaimed for bad debt relief is:	

(b) **Calculate the figure for Box 1 of the VAT return quarter ended 31.12.20X0.**

The figure for Box 1 of the VAT return is:	

(c) **Calculate the figure for Box 4 of the VAT return quarter ended 31.12.20X0.**

The figure for Box 4 of the VAT return is:	

Task 7

This task is about completing a VAT return for Company B.

The following details have been extracted from the company's accounting ledgers:

QUARTER ENDED 31 MARCH 20X0

Sales account

Date	Reference	Debit £	Date	Reference	Credit £
			01.01.20X0-31.03.20X0	Sales day book – UK sales	797,830.00
31.03.20X0	Balance c/d	872,990.00	01.01.20X0-31.03.20X0	Sales day book – zero-rated EU despatches	75,160.00
	Total	872,990.00		Total	872,990.00

Purchases / expenses account

Date	Reference	Debit £	Date	Reference	Credit £
31.03.20X0	Purchases day book	520,565.00	01.01.20X0-31.03.20X0	Balance c/d	520,565.00
	Total	520,565.00		Total	520,565.00

VAT account

Date	Reference	Debit £	Date	Reference	Credit £
01.01.20X0 -31.03.20X0	Purchases day book	104,113.00	01.01.20X0-31.03.20X0	Sales day book	159,566.00

A debt of £606.00, inclusive of VAT, was written-off as irrecoverable (bad) in March 20X0. The related sale was due for payment ten months ago. Bad debt relief is now to be claimed.

Complete boxes 1 to 9 of the VAT return below for quarter ended 31 March 20X0

VAT return for quarter ended 31 March 20X0		£
VAT due in this period on **sales** and other outputs	Box 1	
VAT due in this period on **acquisitions** from other **EC Member States**	Box 2	
Total VAT due (**the sum of boxes 1 and 2**)	Box 3	
VAT reclaimed in this period on **purchases** and other inputs, including acquisitions from the EC	Box 4	
Net VAT to be paid to HM Revenue & Customs or reclaimed by you (**Difference between boxes 3 and 4 – if Box 4 is greater than Box 3, use a minus sign**)	Box 5	
Total value of **sales** and all other outputs excluding any VAT. **Include your box 8 figure. Whole pounds only**	Box 6	
Total value of **purchases** and all other inputs excluding any VAT. **Include your box 9 figure. Whole pounds only**	Box 7	
Total value of all **supplies** of goods and related costs, excluding any VAT, to other **EC Member States. Whole pounds only**	Box 8	
Total value of all **acquisitions** of goods and related costs, excluding any VAT, from other **EC Member States. Whole pounds only**	Box 9	

Task 8

You work in a large company and have just completed the VAT return for the quarter ended 31 March 20X1. The VAT return showed an amount of £8,000.00 in box 1 and in box 3, and an amount of £2,000.00 in box 4.

Complete the memo to the financial controller regarding the payment of VAT for this quarter.

MEMO

To: Financial Controller

From: An Accountant

Subject: VAT payment for the quarter ended 31 March 20X1

Date: 14 April 20X1

The VAT [⯆] is [⯆].We [⯆] this by [⯆].

Picklist:

payable
repayable
£8,000.00
£2,000.00
£6,000.00
must pay
will receive
30 April 20X1
7 May 20X1

....

BPP PRACTICE ASSESSMENT 1
INDIRECT TAX (ITAX – AQ2013)

ANSWERS

Indirect Tax Practice Assessment 1 – Answers

Task 1

(a)

	True	False
Joseph will be in a repayment position if he voluntarily registers	✓	
Julie's customers will not suffer the impact of her charging VAT unless they are not VAT-registered	✓	

(b)

	True	False
Clover Ltd must VAT-register as total turnover exceeds £82,000		✓

Only taxable turnover is considered when determining whether the threshold has been exceeded. Taxable turnover is £74,000.

Task 2

(a) **31 March 20X0**

	✓
Nil	
£40	✓
£360	
£400	

Only the tax point for the deposit falls in quarter ended 31 March 20X0

(b) **30 June 20X0**

	✓
Nil	
£40	
£360	✓
£400	

The basic tax point for the balance would be 22 March 20X0 (date goods are sent), however an invoice is sent within 14 days, making this date (1 April 20X0) the actual tax point.

(c)

	✓
Only the input tax relating to taxable supplies is recoverable, in all circumstances	
All input tax is recoverable if certain de minimis tests are satisfied	✓
No input tax is recoverable	
All input tax is recoverable as no supplies are outside the scope of VAT	

Task 3

(a)

	✓
£945.00	
£1,134.00	✓
£882.00	

(£9,000 × 120%) × 10.5% = £1,134.00

(b)

	✓
More VAT payable if not in the flat rate scheme	✓
Less VAT payable if not in the flat rate scheme	

If not in the flat rate scheme Igor's VAT payable would be:

		£
Output tax	£9,000 × 20%	1,800.00
Input tax	£2,000 × 20%	(400.00)
		1,400.00

As this is more than £1,134.00 Igor would have more VAT payable.

(c)

	✓
Only one VAT return per annum is required	
It helps regulate cash flow	
It reduces the administrative burden on the business	
Only one VAT payment per annum is required	✓

Task 4

(a)

	✓
Nil	
£92.00	
£480.00	✓
£3,372.00	

VAT is irrecoverable on cars with an element of private use and on most business entertaining.

(b)

	True	False
If a trader submits an inaccurate VAT return but tells HMRC of the inaccuracy as soon as possible, this may reduce the possible penalty	✓	
Tax evasion is illegal and may lead to fines and imprisonment	✓	

Task 5

(a)

The amount of VAT on the invoice is	£	22.19

£133.18 × 1/6

(b)

	✓
The VAT payment for the previous period of £5,000.00 was not posted to the VAT account	
The VAT payment for the previous period of £5,000.00 was posted to the wrong side of the VAT account	✓

If the VAT payment for the previous period of £5,000.00 was posted to the wrong side of the VAT account, the liability showing on the account would be £5,000.00 (VAT payable for previous period) + £5,000.00 (VAT paid, but posted to the wrong side) + £18,400.00 (the liability for the current period) = £28,400.00.

If the VAT payment for the previous period of £5,000.00 was not posted to the VAT account, the liability showing on the account would be £5,000.00 (VAT payable for previous period) + £18,400.00 (the liability for the current period) = £23,400.00.

When the VAT payment for the previous period of £5,000.00 is posted to the correct side (the debit side) of the VAT account this will reduce the balance on the VAT account to the correct VAT payable of £18,400.00. as shown below.

VAT ACCOUNT

Date 20X1	Reference	Debit £	Date 20X1	Reference	Credit £
	VAT paid	5,000.00	30.9.20X1	VAT payable	5,000.00
			31.12.20X1	VAT payable	18,400.00
	Balance c/d	18,400.00			
	Total	23,400.00		Total	23,400.00
			31.12.20X1	**VAT payable**	**18,400.00**

Task 6

(a)

The figure to be reclaimed for bad debt relief is:	£126.33

£758 × 1/6 = £126.33

(b)

The figure for Box 1 of the VAT return is:	£14,000.00

(c)

The figure for Box 4 of the VAT return is:	£3,106.33

£3,440.00 − £460.00 + £126.33

Task 7

VAT return for quarter ended 31 March 20X0		£
VAT due in this period on **sales** and other outputs	Box 1	159,566.00
VAT due in this period on **acquisitions** from other **EC Member States**	Box 2	0
Total VAT due (**the sum of boxes 1 and 2**)	Box 3	159,566.00
VAT reclaimed in this period on **purchases** and other inputs, including acquisitions from the EC	Box 4	104,214.00
Net VAT to be paid to HM Revenue & Customs or reclaimed by you (**Difference between boxes 3 and 4 – if Box 4 is greater than Box 3, use a minus sign**)	Box 5	55,352.00
Total value of **sales** and all other outputs excluding any VAT. **Include your box 8 figure. Whole pounds only**	Box 6	872,990
Total value of **purchases** and all other inputs excluding any VAT. **Include your box 9 figure. Whole pounds only**	Box 7	520,565
Total value of all **supplies** of goods and related costs, excluding any VAT, to other **EC Member States. Whole pounds only**	Box 8	75,160
Total value of all **acquisitions** of goods and related costs, excluding any VAT, from other **EC Member States. Whole pounds only**	Box 9	0

Working: Box 4 = £104,113.00 + (£606.00 × 1/6) = £104,214.00

Task 8

	MEMO	
To:	Financial Controller	
From:	An Accountant	
Subject:	VAT payment for the quarter ended 31 March 20X1	
Date:	14 April 20X1	

The VAT [payable ▼] is [£6,000 ▼]. We

[must pay ▼] this by

[7 May 20X1 ▼] .

BPP PRACTICE ASSESSMENT 2
INDIRECT TAX (ITAX – AQ2013)

Time allowed: 1.5 hours

PRACTICE ASSESSMENT 2

Indirect Tax Practice Assessment 2

Task 1 (5 marks)

(a) A VAT-registered manufacturer sold a product to a VAT-registered retailer for £100 plus VAT of £20. The retailer sold the product to a member of the public for £180 including VAT of £30.

Which of the following statements is TRUE? TICK ONE BOX.

	✓
The retailer bears a VAT cost of £20 and the member of public bears a VAT cost of £10.	
The retailer bears a VAT cost of £30.	
The member of the public bears a VAT cost of £30.	
No one bears the VAT cost as the retailer and the member of the public can both reclaim the VAT from HMRC.	

(b) During the first nine months of trade, a business made zero-rated supplies totalling £40,000 and exempt supplies totalling £45,000.

Which of the following statements is TRUE? TICK ONE BOX.

	✓
The trader must register for VAT as his supplies have exceeded the VAT registration threshold	
The trader cannot register for VAT as he does not make any standard-rated supplies	
The trader was automatically registered for VAT as soon as he started trading	
The trader can voluntarily register for VAT as he makes some taxable supplies	

Task 2 (7 marks)

(a) **Identify whether the following statement is True or False.** TICK ONE BOX.

When a trader issues a credit note to a customer it decreases the VAT payable by the trader for that quarter.

True	False

(b) **Identify whether the following statements in relation to VAT invoices are True or False.** TICK ONE BOX ON EACH ROW.

	True	False
A VAT invoice must include certain details including the VAT registration number, the total VAT payable and a description of the goods supplied		
A less detailed (simplified) invoice may be issued if the VAT-exclusive proceeds are no more than £250		
If a sale is made to a VAT-registered customer in the EU, the invoice must include the standard rate of VAT unless the invoice includes the customer's VAT number		

(c) **Which of the following statements is TRUE about a VAT-registered company making both standard-rated and exempt supplies?** TICK ONE BOX.

	✓
No input VAT can be recovered	
All input VAT can always be recovered because the company makes some taxable supplies	
All input VAT can be recovered, provided certain de minimis limits are not exceeded	

Task 3 (5 marks)

Gomez uses the annual accounting scheme for his business. The business's VAT liability for the year ended 30 June 20X0 was £15,000 and for the following year, the year ended 30 June 20X1, it was £18,500.

(a) **The final balancing payment for the year ended 30 June 20X1 is:**

TICK ONE BOX.

	✓
£Nil	
£3,500	
£5,000	
£18,500	

(b) **The final balancing payment is due by:**

TICK ONE BOX.

	✓
30 June 20X1	
30 July 20X1	
31 July 20X1	
31 August 20X1	

(c) Xavier has a quarter ended 31 December 20X0. His normal payment terms are one calendar month after invoice date.

Identify whether bad debt relief can be claimed in respect of the following amounts owed to Xavier as at 31 December 20X0.

Moraira Ltd owes £3,000 from an invoice issued on 2 January 20X0. Xavier believes that the amount will be paid in full and so it has not been written-off in the accounts.

TICK ONE BOX.

	✓
Bad debt relief can be claimed	
Bad debt relief cannot be claimed	

Calpe Ltd owes £2,000 from an invoice issued on 15 June 20X0. Xavier does not expect that the amount will be paid and so it has been written-off in the accounts.

TICK ONE BOX.

	✓
Bad debt relief can be claimed	
Bad debt relief cannot be claimed	

Task 4 (7 marks)

(a) **Failing to register for VAT at the right time may lead to:**

TICK ONE BOX.

	✓
A surcharge liability notice	
A surcharge	
A penalty	
No consequences	

(b) Claudia deliberately understated her output VAT on her last return but now she wishes to correct this.

Identify which one of the following statements is the correct action Claudia must take to correct the error.

TICK ONE BOX.

	✓
The error can be adjusted for on the next return, but Claudia must also inform HMRC separately and she may be liable to a penalty	
The error cannot be adjusted on the next return, so Claudia must inform HMRC separately in writing, and will not be liable to a penalty	
The error cannot be adjusted on the next return, so Claudia must inform HMRC separately in writing, and may also be liable to a penalty	

(c) **Identify whether the following statement is True or False.**

The VAT fuel scale charge is the amount of input tax recoverable on private fuel purchases.

TICK ONE BOX.

True	False

Task 5 (6 marks)

(a) **Complete the table below by inserting figures into the blank boxes.**

Net £	VAT @ 20% £	Gross £
		270.60
260.00		

(b) A business has completed its VAT return, which shows a correct amount of £5,600.00 owing to HMRC. The VAT account at the end of the same period shows a liability of £8,000.00.

Which of the following could explain this difference? TICK ONE BOX.

	✓
The VAT payment for the previous period of £2,400 has not been entered in the VAT account	
The VAT payment for the previous period of £2,400 has been entered twice in the VAT account	

Task 6 (6 marks)

The following accounts have been extracted from the ledger accounts of Joseph Marselus for period ended 31 March 20X0.

Sales are made at the standard rate.

Sales and sales return account

Date 20X0	Reference	Debit £	Date 20X0	Reference	Credit £
01.01-31.03	Sales returns day book – UK sales returns	13,000.00	01.01-31.03	Sales day book – UK sales	275,000.00
31.03	Balance c/d	262,000.00			
	Total	275,000.00		Total	275,000.00

Purchases account

Date 20X0	Reference	Debit £	Date 20X0	Reference	Credit £
01.01-31.03	Purchases day book – UK purchases	101,000.00	31.03	Balance c/d	101,000.00
	Total	101,000.00		Total	101,000.00

VAT account

Date 20X0	Reference	Debit £	Date 20X0	Reference	Credit £
01.01-31.03	Sales returns day book	2,600.00	01.01-31.03	Sales day book	55,000.00
01.01-31.03	Purchases day book	20,200.00			

Joseph Marselus accidentally left out a couple of invoices from his last VAT return.

- Invoice 1 was for £3,400.00 (VAT-exclusive) to a customer
- Invoice 2 was for £254.00 (VAT-exclusive) from a supplier

He is able to correct them on his next return.

(a) **Calculate the net VAT adjustment figure needed to correct these errors.**

£ [   ]

(b) **Calculate the figure for Box 1 of the VAT Return.**

£ [   ]

(c) **Calculate the figure for Box 4 of the VAT Return.**

£ [   ]

Task 7 (17 marks)

The following accounts have been extracted from Gilbert Jones Ltd's ledgers for the period August to October 20X0.

Sales account

Date	Reference	Debit £	Date	Reference	Credit £
			01.08.20X0-31.10.20X0	Sales day book – UK standard-rated sales	561,932.00
31.10.20X0	Balance c/d	591,329.00	01.08.20X0-31.10.20X0	Sales day book – zero-rated EU despatches	29,397.00
	Total	591,329.00		Total	591,329.00

Purchases/expenses account

Date	Reference	Debit £	Date	Reference	Credit £
01.08.20X0-31.10.20X0	Purchases day book – UK standard-rated expenses	192,912.00			
01.08.20X0-31.10.20X0	Purchases day book – EU acquisitions – standard-rated	15,400.00	31.10.20X0	Balance c/d	208,312.00
	Total	208,312.00		Total	208,312.00

VAT account

Date	Reference	Debit £	Date	Reference	Credit £
01.08.20X0-31.10.20X0	Purchases day book	41,662.40	01.08.20X0-31.10.20X0	Sales day book	112,386.40

Complete boxes 1 to 9 of the VAT return below for quarter ended 31 October 20X0

VAT return for quarter ended 31 October 20X0		£
VAT due in this period on **sales** and other outputs	Box 1	
VAT due in this period on **acquisitions** from other **EC Member States**	Box 2	
Total VAT due (**the sum of boxes 1 and 2**)	Box 3	
VAT reclaimed in this period on **purchases** and other inputs, including acquisitions from the EC	Box 4	
Net VAT to be paid to HM Revenue & Customs or reclaimed by you (**Difference between boxes 3 and 4 – if Box 4 is greater than Box 3, use a minus sign**)	Box 5	
Total value of **sales** and all other outputs excluding any VAT. **Include your box 8 figure. Whole pounds only**	Box 6	
Total value of **purchases** and all other inputs excluding any VAT. **Include your box 9 figure. Whole pounds only**	Box 7	
Total value of all **supplies** of goods and related costs, excluding any VAT, to other **EC Member States. Whole pounds only**	Box 8	
Total value of all **acquisitions** of goods and related costs, excluding any VAT, from other **EC Member States. Whole pounds only**	Box 9	

Task 8 (7 marks)

You work for a firm of accountants. One of your clients, Donald Smith Ltd, has provided you with the following information. It is 12 Nov 20X0.

The showroom of Donald Smith Ltd sold some goods for £15,000 plus VAT to a customer, GHA Stores plc, in February 20X0 on 30 days' credit. Donald Smith Ltd was informed yesterday that GHA Stores plc had ceased trading and the debt is irrecoverable. This is the first time that Donald Smith Ltd has had a substantial bad debt. Donald Smith Ltd has a VAT registration number of 482 912 5407.

You are required to write to Donald Smith Ltd, explaining the steps that Donald Smith Ltd needs to take in order to claim bad debt relief for the VAT element of this debt, and the timescale in which the steps should be taken so that relief is obtained as soon as possible. Donald Smith Ltd's next VAT return will be for the quarter ending 31 January 20X1.

ABC Accountants

Tate House, Henry Road, Guildford, Surrey. GU8 5CM

Telephone: 01344 627896

Donald Smith Ltd
Park Drive Trading Estate
Sunninghill Road
Ascot
Berks
BU8 5ZD

12 November 20X0

Dear Sirs

I understand you have recently been informed that a net sale of £ [▼] to GHA Stores plc in February on 30 days' credit is now a bad debt.

The steps set out below will enable you to claim bad debt relief for the VAT element of the debt (£ [▼]) in your next VAT return.

- Write off the entire debt of £ [▼] in your accounts before 31 January 20X1

- Retain a copy of the VAT invoice and the journal writing it off

- In your next VAT return, for the quarter ending 31 January 20X1 (when the debt will be more than [▼] months overdue), add £ [▼] to Box [▼] (input tax box).

If you have any further queries please do not hesitate to contact me.

Yours faithfully

Deputy Accountant

Picklist:

£3,000.00
£18,000
£3,600.00
£21,600
£15,000
£3,000.00
12
6
1
4

BPP PRACTICE ASSESSMENT 2
INDIRECT TAX (ITAX – AQ2013)

ANSWERS

Indirect Tax Practice Assessment 2 – Answers

Task 1

(a)

	✓
The retailer bears a VAT cost of £20 and the member of public bears a VAT cost of £10.	
The retailer bears a VAT cost of £30.	
The member of the public bears a VAT cost of £30.	✓
No one bears the VAT cost as the retailer and the member of the public can both reclaim the VAT from HMRC.	

(b)

	✓
The trader must register for VAT as his supplies have exceeded the VAT registration threshold	
The trader cannot register for VAT as he does not make any standard-rated supplies	
The trader was automatically registered for VAT as soon as he started trading	
The trader can voluntarily register for VAT as he makes some taxable supplies	✓

Task 2

(a)

True	False
✓	

A sales credit note decreases the VAT payable.

(b)

	True	False
A VAT invoice must include certain details including the VAT registration number, the total VAT payable and a description of the goods supplied	✓	
A less detailed (simplified) invoice may be issued if the VAT exclusive proceeds are no more than £250		✓
If a sale is made to a VAT-registered customer in the EU, the invoice must include the standard rate of VAT unless the invoice includes the customer's VAT number	✓	

A less detailed (simplified) invoice may be issued if the VAT *inclusive* proceeds are no more than £250

(c)

	✓
No input VAT can be recovered	
All input VAT can always be recovered because the company makes some taxable supplies	
All input VAT can be recovered, provided certain de minimis limits are not exceeded	✓

- -

Task 3

(a)

	✓
£Nil	
£3,500	
£5,000	✓
£18,500	

£18,500 − (£15,000 × 10% × 9)

(b)

	✓
30 June 20X1	
30 July 20X1	
31 July 20X1	
31 August 20X1	✓

Within two months of VAT annual period.

(c) Moraira Ltd

	✓
Bad debt relief can be claimed	
Bad debt relief cannot be claimed	✓

The debt has not been written off in the accounts

Calpe Ltd

	✓
Bad debt relief can be claimed	
Bad debt relief cannot be claimed	✓

It is less than six months since the debt was due for payment (15 July 20X0)

Task 4

(a)

	✓
A surcharge liability notice	
A surcharge	
A penalty	✓
No consequences	

(b)

	✓
The error can be adjusted for on the next return, but Claudia must also inform HMRC separately and she may be liable to a penalty	
The error cannot be adjusted on the next return, so Claudia must inform HMRC separately in writing, and will not be liable to a penalty	
The error cannot be adjusted on the next return, so Claudia must inform HMRC separately in writing, and may also be liable to a penalty	✓

(c)

True	False
	✓

The fuel scale charge is an amount of output tax to offset against the input tax reclaimed on fuel purchase invoices.

Task 5

(a)

Net £	VAT @ 20% £	Gross £
225.50	45.10	270.60
260.00	52.00	312.00

£270.60 × 1/6 = £45.10

£260.00 × 20% = £52.00

(b)

	✓
The VAT payment for the previous period of £2,400 has not been entered in the VAT account	✓
The VAT payment for the previous period of £2,400 has been entered twice in the VAT account	

If the payment for the previous period had been posted in the VAT account, the liability showing would be £8,000.00 − £2,400.00 = £5,600.00, ie the liability for the current period.

If the previous payment had been entered twice, the balance showing on the VAT account would have been too low by £2,400.00, ie would have been £3,200.00.

Task 6

(a)

£	629.20

($3,400 \times 20\%$) – ($254 \times 20\%$)

(b) **Box 1 of the VAT Return.**

£	53,029.20

£55,000.00 – £2,600.00 + net error £629.20

If there is more than one error, they are netted off, and one adjustment is made. Here there is a net understatement of output tax and so the figure in box 1 is increased.

(c) **Box 4 of the VAT Return.**

£	20,200.00

Task 7

VAT return for quarter ended 31 October 20X0		£
VAT due in this period on **sales** and other outputs	Box 1	112,386.40
VAT due in this period on **acquisitions** from other **EC Member States**	Box 2	3,080.00
Total VAT due (**the sum of boxes 1 and 2**)	Box 3	115,466.40
VAT reclaimed in this period on **purchases** and other inputs, including acquisitions from the EC	Box 4	41,662.40
Net VAT to be paid to HM Revenue & Customs or reclaimed by you (**Difference between boxes 3 and 4 – if Box 4 is greater than Box 3, use a minus sign**)	Box 5	73,804.00
Total value of **sales** and all other outputs excluding any VAT. **Include your box 8 figure. Whole pounds only**	Box 6	591,329
Total value of **purchases** and all other inputs excluding any VAT. **Include your box 9 figure. Whole pounds only**	Box 7	208,312
Total value of all **supplies** of goods and related costs, excluding any VAT, to other **EC Member States. Whole pounds only**	Box 8	29,397
Total value of all **acquisitions** of goods and related costs, excluding any VAT, from other **EC Member States. Whole pounds only**	Box 9	15,400

Task 8

ABC Accountants

Tate House, Henry Road, Guildford, Surrey. GU8 5CM

Telephone: 01344 627896

Donald Smith Ltd
Park Drive Trading Estate
Sunninghill Road
Ascot
Berks
BU8 5ZD

12 November 20X0

Dear Sirs

I understand you have recently been informed that a net sale of £ | 15,000 ▼ | to GHA Stores plc in February on 30 days' credit is now a bad debt.

The steps set out below will enable you to claim bad debt relief for the VAT element of the debt (£ | 3,000.00 ▼ |) in your next VAT return.

- Write off the entire debt of £ | 18,000 ▼ | in your accounts before 31 January 20X1

- Retain a copy of the VAT invoice and the journal writing it off

- In your next VAT return, for the quarter ending 31 January 20X1 (when the debt will be more than | 6 ▼ | months overdue), add £ | 3,000.00 ▼ | to Box | 4 ▼ | (input tax box).

If you have any further queries please do not hesitate to contact me.

Yours faithfully

Deputy Accountant

· ·

BPP PRACTICE ASSESSMENT 3
INDIRECT TAX (ITAX – AQ2013)

Time allowed: 1.5 hours

Indirect Tax Practice Assessment 3

Task 1 (5 marks)

(a) It is 31 December, Julian has been trading for ten months and his taxable turnover has consistently been £7,500 per month. Next month's turnover is expected to be the same.

Indicate whether Julian should register for VAT immediately, in the next 30 days or monitor his turnover and register later. TICK ONE BOX.

	✓
Register immediately	
Register in next 30 days	
Monitor turnover and register later	

(b) It is 31 December, Jasper has been trading for ten months and his taxable turnover has consistently been £6,500 per month. Next month he is expecting additional payment of £76,000, in addition to his normal monthly turnover.

Indicate whether Julian should register for VAT immediately, in the next 30 days or monitor his turnover and register later. TICK ONE BOX.

	✓
Register immediately	
Register in next 30 days	
Monitor turnover and register later	

Task 2 (7 marks)

Identify for the two statements below whether they are True or False.

(a) When a VAT-registered trader who makes standard-rated supplies receives a credit note from a supplier, VAT payable by the trader will increase.

TICK ONE BOX.

	✓
TRUE	
FALSE	

(b) A business makes supplies that are both standard-rated and zero-rated. All of the input VAT can be reclaimed providing certain de minimis conditions are met.

TICK ONE BOX.

	✓
TRUE	
FALSE	

(c) A registered trader receives an order for goods on 15 June 20X1. The trader delivers the goods to the customer on 20 June 20X1, and issues an invoice on 23 June 20X1. The customer pays for the goods in full on 2 July 20X1.

Identify the tax point for this transaction.

TICK ONE BOX.

	✓
15 June 20X1	
20 June 20X1	
23 June 20X1	
2 July 20X1	

(d) **Identify with a tick which TWO of the following does not need to be included on a valid VAT invoice.**

	✓
VAT number of supplier	
Invoice date	
VAT number of customer	
Rate of VAT	
Total price excluding VAT for each type of item	
Total amount of VAT for each type of item	
Total price including VAT for each type of item	
Name and address of customer	
Name and address of supplier	

Task 3 (5 marks)

(a) A business operates the cash accounting scheme

Indicate which one of the following statements would be a benefit of using this scheme. TICK ONE BOX.

	✓
Only having to submit one VAT return a year	
Automatic bad debt relief	
Paying a percentage of turnover over to HMRC	

(b) A business operates the annual accounting scheme.

Indicate which one of the following statements would be correct when using this scheme. TICK ONE BOX.

	✓
Each year, the business submits one annual return and makes one payment	
Each year, the business submits one annual return and makes ten payments	
Each year, the business submits one annual return and makes five payments	

(c) A business operates the flat rate scheme.

Indicate which one of the following statements would be correct when using this scheme. TICK ONE BOX.

	✓
The business pays a percentage of tax-inclusive turnover to HMRC and reclaims input VAT	
The business pays a percentage of tax-exclusive turnover to HMRC and reclaims input VAT	
The business pays a percentage of tax-inclusive turnover to HMRC and cannot reclaim input VAT	
The business pays a percentage of tax-exclusive turnover to HMRC and cannot reclaim input VAT	

Task 4 (7 marks)

(a) Vince is an employee of Brown Ltd and he has the use of a company car which he uses both privately and for business. Brown Ltd pays for all the petrol costs on the car for the quarter and recovers all the input tax on these costs.

Which of the following statements is TRUE? TICK ONE BOX.

	✓
Brown Ltd must charge an amount of output tax (the fuel scale charge) to reflect the private use	
Brown Ltd must charge an amount of input tax (the fuel scale charge) to reflect the private use	

(b) Victoria made an error on her last VAT return. She cannot correct the error on her current VAT return, instead she needs to inform HMRC in writing preferably by completing form 652 "Notification of Errors in VAT Returns".

Identify with a tick any of the following statements that could be correct in relation to this error.

	✓
The error is less than the error correction reporting threshold, but deliberate	
The error is less than the error correction reporting threshold, but not deliberate	
The error is more than the error correction reporting threshold, and deliberate	
The error is more than the error correction reporting threshold, but not deliberate	

(c) **Identify for the two statements below whether they are True or False**

A VAT-registered trader importing goods from outside the EU must charge himself the output VAT due on those goods, but will also treat it as input VAT on the same VAT return, resulting in a net effect of nil.

TICK ONE BOX.

	✓
TRUE	
FALSE	

Goods exported to a country outside the EU will normally be treated as exempt supplies.

TICK ONE BOX.

	✓
TRUE	
FALSE	

Task 5 (6 marks)

(a) A VAT-registered pet shop makes the following mixed supply:

- Exempt items for £256.98
- Zero-rated items for £85.73
- Standard-rated items for £796.53 plus VAT

How much should the trader include as output VAT on its VAT return in respect of this supply?

TICK ONE BOX.

	✓
£132.75	
£176.45	
£159.30	
£159.31	

(b) The VAT account at the end of a period shows the correct VAT liability of £3,000.00. The VAT return shows a liability of £3,600.00.

Which of the following could explain the difference.

TICK ONE BOX.

	✓
Bad debt relief (VAT of £300.00) has been included as output tax rather than input tax on the return	
A VAT refund from the previous period of £600.00 has been included as input tax on the VAT return	

Task 6 (6 marks)

The following summaries have been extracted from the accounts of Guy LeBlond over a three month period.

The business's EU acquisitions are goods that would normally be standard-rated.

Sales day-book summary

	Zero-rated sales	Standard-rated sales	VAT	Total
UK sales	42,500.00	567,000.00	113,400.00	722,900.00

Purchases day-book summary

	Zero-rated purchases	Standard-rated purchases	VAT – on UK purchases	EU acquisitions	Total
UK purchases/expenses	4,250.00	150,600.00	30,120.00	25,678.00	210,648.00

(a) **Calculate the figure for Box 1 of the VAT Return.**

£ _____

(b) **Calculate the figure for Box 2 of the VAT Return.**

£ _____

(c) **Calculate the figure for Box 4 of the VAT Return.**

£ _____

Task 7 (17 marks)

The following accounts have been extracted from Bradley Ltd's ledgers for quarter ended 30 June 20X1.

Sales and sales returns account

Date	Reference	Debit £	Date	Reference	Credit £
01.04.20X1-30.06.20X1	Sales returns day book – UK standard-rated sales	3,700.00	01.04.20X1-30.06.20X1	Sales day book – UK standard-rated sales	67,000.00
30.06.20X1	Balance c/d	85,800.00	01.04.20X1-30.06.20X1	Sales day book – UK zero-rated sales	22,500.00
	Total	89,500.00		Total	89,500.00

Purchases account

Date	Reference	Debit £	Date	Reference	Credit £
01.04.20X1-30.06.20X1	Purchases day book – UK standard-rated purchases	15,600.00			
01.04.20X1-30.06.20X1	Purchases day book – UK zero-rated purchases	4,250.00			
01.04.20X1-30.06.20X1	Cash book – UK purchases	8,550.00	30.06.20X1	Balance c/d	28,400.00
	Total	28,400.00		Total	28,400.00

VAT account

Date	Reference	Debit £	Date	Reference	Credit £
01.04.20X1-30.06.20X1	Purchases day book	3,120.00	01.04.20X1-30.06.20X1	Sales day book	13,400.00
01.04.20X1-30.06.20X1	Sales returns day book	740.00			
01.04.20X1-30.06.20X1	Cash book	1,710.00			

Journal (extract)

	Debit £	Credit £
Irrecoverable (bad) debts expense	5,200.00	
VAT account	1,040.00	
Receivables (debtors) (VAT-inclusive at 20 %)		6,240.00

Complete boxes 1 to 9 of the VAT return below for quarter ended 30 June 20X1

VAT return for quarter ended 30 June 20X1		£
VAT due in this period on **sales** and other outputs	**Box 1**	
VAT due in this period on **acquisitions** from other **EC Member States**	**Box 2**	
Total VAT due (**the sum of boxes 1 and 2**)	**Box 3**	
VAT reclaimed in this period on **purchases** and other inputs, including acquisitions from the EC	**Box 4**	
Net VAT to be paid to HM Revenue & Customs or reclaimed by you (**Difference between boxes 3 and 4 – if Box 4 is greater than Box 3, use a minus sign**)	**Box 5**	
Total value of **sales** and all other outputs excluding any VAT. **Include your box 8 figure. Whole pounds only**	**Box 6**	
Total value of **purchases** and all other inputs excluding any VAT. **Include your box 9 figure. Whole pounds only**	**Box 7**	

VAT return for quarter ended 30 June 20X1		£
Total value of all **supplies** of goods and related costs, excluding any VAT, to other **EC Member States. Whole pounds only**	Box 8	
Total value of all **acquisitions** of goods and related costs, excluding any VAT, from other **EC Member States. Whole pounds only**	Box 9	

Task 8 (7 marks)

Reply to Holly Field's email giving her the information she has requested

To: Accounts assistant

From: Holly Field

Subject: Impact of a rise in the VAT rate

Date: 17 July 20X1

I have been listening to the news recently and have heard there may be a rise in the standard rate of VAT from 20% to 25%.

I am extremely concerned as to how this will affect my business. Most of my sales are direct to the general public, so I am unsure whether to increase my prices to take account of the proposed new rate, or to try and keep them the same.

Would you mind explaining the consequences of these two options for me?

Your speedy response would be much appreciated.

Holly

You are required to reply to Holly, filling in the missing details of the email below.

EMAIL

To:	Holly Field
From:	Accounts assistant
Subject:	Impact of a rise in the VAT rate
Date:	20 July 20X1

Dear Holly,

Thank you for your email requesting details of how the proposed rise in the standard rate of VAT might affect your business.

As you quite rightly say, you [_____ ▼], which means effectively, you as a business will suffer the impact of the increased rate. Alternatively you could [_____ ▼] resulting in your customers having to pay extra, which in itself, may lead to the loss of revenue.

For example with the present rate of VAT at 20%, if you want to make income of £100 on a sale, you will charge your customers [_____ ▼].

With a proposed rise to 25% you can either:

- [_____ ▼] to your customer, which will still leave you £100; or

- [_____ ▼] for your customers, leaving you only £96 after output VAT is charged (£120 × 100/125).

This is a decision that you will need to give careful thought to, but I hope this clarifies the situation for you.

Kind regards

Accounts Assistant

Picklist:

increase your prices
could keep your prices the same
£100.
£120.
charge £125 (£100 plus 25% VAT)
keep your price at £120

BPP PRACTICE ASSESSMENT 3
INDIRECT TAX (ITAX – AQ2013)

ANSWERS

Indirect Tax Practice Assessment 3 – Answers

Task 1

(a)

	✓
Register immediately	
Register in next 30 days	
Monitor turnover and register later	✓

(b)

	✓
Register immediately	✓
Register in next 30 days	
Monitor turnover and register later	

Task 2

(a) When a VAT-registered trader who makes standard-rated supplies receives a credit note from a supplier, VAT payable by the trader will increase.

	✓
TRUE	✓
FALSE	

(b) The de minimis test is applied when a trader makes taxable and *exempt* supplies.

A business that makes supplies that are standard-rated and zero-rated (both taxable supplies) can reclaim all its input without applying any tests.

	✓
TRUE	
FALSE	✓

(c) The basic tax point (delivery date) of 20 June is replaced by the actual tax point (invoice date) of 23 June as the invoice is issued within 14 days of the basic tax point.

	✓
15 June 20X1	
20 June 20X1	
23 June 20X1	✓
2 July 20X1	

(d)

	✓
VAT number of supplier	
Invoice date	
VAT number of customer	✓
Rate of VAT	
Total price excluding VAT for each type of item	
Total amount of VAT for each type of item	
Total price including VAT for each type of item	✓
Name and address of customer	
Name and address of supplier	

Task 3

(a) A business operating the cash accounting scheme will benefit from:

	✓
Only having to submit one VAT return a year	
Automatic bad debt relief	✓
Paying a percentage of turnover over to HMRC	

(b) When a business operates the annual accounting scheme:

	✓
Each year, the business submits one annual return and makes one payment	
Each year, the business submits one annual return and makes ten payments	✓
Each year, the business submits one annual return and makes five payments	

(c) When a business operating the flat rate scheme:

	✓
The business pays a percentage of tax-inclusive turnover to HMRC and reclaims input VAT	
The business pays a percentage of tax-exclusive turnover to HMRC and reclaims input VAT	
The business pays a percentage of tax-inclusive turnover to HMRC and cannot reclaim input VAT	✓
The business pays a percentage of tax-exclusive turnover to HMRC and cannot reclaim input VAT	

....

Task 4

(a)

	✓
Brown Ltd must charge an amount of output tax (the fuel scale charge) to reflect the private use	✓
Brown Ltd must charge an amount of input tax (the fuel scale charge) to reflect the private use	

(b)

	✓
The error is less than the error correction reporting threshold, but deliberate	✓
The error is less than the error correction reporting threshold, but not deliberate	
The error is more than the error correction reporting threshold, and deliberate	✓
The error is more than the error correction reporting threshold, but not deliberate	✓

(c)

	✓
TRUE	
FALSE	✓

The statement describes the action a trader must take when 'acquiring' goods from within the EU.

	✓
TRUE	
FALSE	✓

Goods exported to a country outside the EU will normally be treated as zero-rated supplies.

Task 5

(a) 796.53 x 20% = 159.30 (rounded down)

	✓
£132.75	
£176.45	
£159.30	✓
£159.31	

(b)

	✓
Bad debt relief (VAT of £300.00) has been included as output tax rather than input tax on the return	✓
A VAT refund from the previous period of £600.00 has been included as input tax on the VAT return	

Task 6

(a) **Box 1 of the VAT Return.**

£ | 113,400.00

(b) **Box 2 of the VAT Return.**

£ | 5,135.60

£25,678.00 × 20%

(c) **Box 4 of the VAT Return.**

£ | 35,255.60

£30,120.00 + £5,135.60

Task 7

VAT return for quarter ended 30 June 20X1		£
VAT due in this period on **sales** and other outputs	Box 1	12,660.00
VAT due in this period on **acquisitions** from other **EC Member States**	Box 2	0
Total VAT due (**the sum of boxes 1 and 2**)	Box 3	12,660.00
VAT reclaimed in this period on **purchases** and other inputs, including acquisitions from the EC	Box 4	5,870.00
Net VAT to be paid to HM Revenue & Customs or reclaimed by you (**Difference between boxes 3 and 4 – if Box 4 is greater than Box 3, use a minus sign**)	Box 5	6,790.00
Total value of **sales** and all other outputs excluding any VAT. **Include your box 8 figure. Whole pounds only**	Box 6	85,800
Total value of **purchases** and all other inputs excluding any VAT. **Include your box 9 figure. Whole pounds only**	Box 7	28,400
Total value of all **supplies** of goods and related costs, excluding any VAT, to other **EC Member States. Whole pounds only**	Box 8	0
Total value of all **acquisitions** of goods and related costs, excluding any VAT, from other **EC Member States. Whole pounds only**	Box 9	0

Workings:

£

Box 1	Sales day-book	13,400.00
	Sales returns day book	(740.00)
		12,660.00
Box 4	Purchases day-book	3,120.00
	Cash payments book	1,710.00
	Bad debt relief	1,040.00
		5,870.00

Task 8

EMAIL

To: Holly Field

From: Accounts assistant

Subject: Impact of a rise in the VAT rate

Date: 20 July 20X1

Dear Holly,

Thank you for your email requesting details of how the proposed rise in the standard rate of VAT might affect your business.

As you quite rightly say, you | could keep your prices the same ▼ | , which means effectively, you as a business will suffer the impact of the increased rate.

Alternatively you could | increase your prices ▼ | resulting in your customers having to pay extra, which in itself, may lead to the loss of revenue.

For example with the present rate of VAT at 20%, if you want to make income of £100 on a sale, you will charge your customers £ | 120 ▼ | .

With a proposed rise to 25% you can either:

- | charge £125 (£100 plus 25% VAT) ▼ | to your customer, which will still leave you £100; or

- | keep your price at £120 ▼ | for your customers, leaving you only £96 after output VAT is charged (£120 × 100/125).

This is a decision that you will need to give careful thought to, but I hope this clarifies the situation for you.

Kind regards

Accounts Assistant

INDEX

Accounting Qualification

Indirect Tax (Level 3)
Reference material

Finance Act 2015 – for assessment 1 January – 31 December 2016

The Association of Accounting Technicians

REFERENCE MATERIAL FOR AAT ASSESSMENT OF INDIRECT TAX

Introduction

This document comprises data that you may need to consult during your Indirect Tax computer-based assessment.

The material can be consulted during the sample and live assessments through pop-up windows. It is made available here so you can familiarise yourself with the content before the test.

Do not take a print of this document into the exam room with you*.

This document may be changed to reflect periodical updates in the computer-based assessment, so please check you have the most recent version while studying. This version is based on Finance Act 2015 and is for use in AAT assessments 1 January – 31 December 2016.

*Unless you need a printed version as part of reasonable adjustments for particular needs, in which case you must discuss this with your tutor at least six weeks before the assessment date.

CONTENTS

INTRODUCTION TO VAT

VAT is a tax that's charged on most goods and services that VAT-registered businesses provide in the UK. It's also charged on goods and some services that are imported from countries outside the European Union (EU), and brought into the UK from other EU countries.

VAT is charged when a VAT-registered business sells taxable goods and services to either another business or to a non-business customer. This is called output tax.

When a VAT-registered business buys taxable goods or services for business use it can generally reclaim the VAT it has paid. This is called input tax.

Her Majesty's Revenue and Customs (HMRC) is the government department responsible for operating the VAT system. Payments of VAT collected are made by VAT-registered businesses to HMRC.

RATES OF VAT

There are three rates of VAT, depending on the goods or services the business provides. The rates are:

- Standard – 20%. The standard-rate VAT fraction for calculating the VAT element of a gross supply is 20/120 or 1/6

- Reduced – 5%.

- Zero – 0%

There are also some goods and services that are:

- Exempt from VAT
- Outside the scope of VAT (outside the UK VAT system altogether)

Taxable supplies

Zero-rated goods and services count as taxable supplies and are part of taxable turnover, but no VAT is added to the selling price because the VAT rate is 0%.

If the business sells goods and services that are exempt, no VAT is added as they're not taxable supplies and they're also not taxable turnover.

Generally, a business can't register for VAT or reclaim the VAT on purchases if it only sells exempt goods and services. Where some of its supplies are of exempt goods and services, the business is referred to as partially exempt. It may not be able to reclaim the VAT on all of its purchases.

A business which buys and sells only – or mainly – zero-rated goods or services can apply to HMRC to be exempt from registering for VAT. This could make sense if the business pays little or no VAT on purchases.

Taxable turnover

Taxable turnover (or taxable outputs) consists of standard-rated sales plus all reduced-rated and zero-rated sales but excludes the VAT on those sales, exempt sales and out-of-scope sales.

REGISTRATION AND DEREGISTRATION THRESHOLDS

Registration threshold

If, as at the end of any month, taxable turnover for the previous 12 months is more than the current registration threshold of £82,000, the business must register for VAT within 30 days. Registration without delay is required if, at any time, the value of taxable turnover in the next 30 day period alone is expected to be more than the registration threshold.

A business which has trading that temporarily takes it above the registration threshold of £82,000 but which expects that turnover to drop back and remain below the deregistration threshold of £80,000 almost immediately can apply for a registration exception. The business must be able to prove to HMRC that the momentary increase is a true one-off occurrence.

If trading is below the registration threshold

If taxable turnover hasn't crossed the registration threshold, the business can still apply to register for VAT voluntarily.

Deregistration threshold

The deregistration threshold is £80,000. If taxable turnover for the year is less than or equal to £80,000, or if it is expected to fall to £80,000 or less in the next 12 months, the business can either:

- Stay registered for VAT, or
- Ask HMRC for its VAT registration to be cancelled.

KEEPING BUSINESS RECORDS AND VAT RECORDS

All VAT-registered businesses must keep certain business and VAT records.

These records are not required to be kept in a set way, provided they:

- Are complete and up-to-date

- Allow the correct amount of VAT owed to HMRC or by HMRC to be worked out

- Are easily accessible when an HMRC visit takes place, eg the figures used to fill in the VAT Return must be easy to find

Business records

Business records which must be kept include the following:

- Annual accounts, including income statements
- Bank statements and paying-in slips
- Cash books and other account books
- Orders and delivery notes
- Purchases and sales day books
- Records of daily takings such as till rolls
- Relevant business correspondence

VAT records

In addition to these business records, VAT records must be kept.

In general, the business must keep the following VAT records:

- Records of all the standard-rated, reduced-rated, zero-rated and exempt goods and services that are bought and sold.

- Copies of all sales invoices issued. However, businesses do not have to keep copies of any less detailed (simplified) VAT invoices for no more than £250 including VAT.

- All purchase invoices for items purchased for business purposes unless the gross value of the supply is £25 or less and the purchase was from a coin-operated telephone or vending machine, or for car parking charges or tolls.

- All credit notes and debit notes received.

- Copies of all credit notes and debit notes issued.

- Records of any goods or services bought for which there is no VAT reclaim, such as business entertainment.

292

- Records of any goods exported.

- Any adjustments, such as corrections to the accounts or amended VAT invoices.

Generally all business records that are relevant for VAT must be kept for at least six years. If this causes serious problems in terms of storage or costs, then HMRC may allow some records to be kept for a shorter period. Records may be stored digitally especially if that is needed to overcome storage and access difficulties.

Keeping a VAT account

A VAT account is the separate record that must be kept of the VAT charged on taxable sales (referred to as output tax or VAT payable) and the VAT paid on purchases (called input tax or VAT reclaimable). It provides the link between the business records and the VAT Return. A VAT-registered business needs to add up the VAT in the sales and purchases records and then transfer these totals to the VAT account, using separate headings for VAT payable and VAT reclaimable.

The VAT account can be kept in whatever way suits the business best, as long as it includes information about the VAT that it:

- Owes on sales
- Owes on acquisitions from other European Union (EU) countries
- Owes following a correction or error adjustment
- Can reclaim on business purchases
- Can reclaim on acquisitions from other EU countries
- Can reclaim following a correction or error adjustment
- Is reclaiming via VAT bad debt relief

The business must also keep records of any adjustments that have been made, such as balancing payments for the annual accounting scheme for VAT.

Information from the VAT account can be used to complete the VAT Return at the end of each accounting period. VAT reclaimable is subtracted from the VAT payable, to give the net amount of VAT to pay to or reclaim from HMRC.

Unless it is using the cash accounting scheme, a business must pay the VAT charged on invoices to customers during the accounting period that relates to the return, even if those customers have not paid the invoices.

EXEMPT AND PARTLY-EXEMPT BUSINESSES

Exempt goods and services

There are some goods and services on which VAT is not charged.

Exempt supplies are not taxable for VAT, so sales of exempt goods and services are not included in taxable turnover for VAT purposes. If a registered business buys exempt items, there is no VAT to reclaim.

(This is different to zero-rated supplies. In both cases VAT is not added to the selling price, but zero-rated goods or services are taxable for VAT at 0%, and are included in taxable turnover.)

Businesses which only sell or supply exempt goods or services

A business which only supplies goods or services that are exempt from VAT is called an exempt business. It cannot register for VAT, so it won't be able to reclaim any input tax on business purchases.

(Again this is different to zero-rated supplies, as a business can reclaim the input tax on any purchases that relate to zero-rated sales. In addition, a business which sells mainly or only zero-rated items may apply for an exemption from VAT registration, but then it can't claim back any input tax.)

Reclaiming VAT in a partly-exempt business

A business that is registered for VAT but that makes some exempt supplies is referred to as partly, or partially, exempt.

Generally, such businesses won't be able to reclaim the input tax paid on purchases that relate to exempt supplies.

However if the amount of input tax incurred relating to exempt supplies is below a minimum de minimis amount, input tax can be reclaimed in full.

If the amount of input tax incurred relating to exempt supplies is above the de minimis amount, only the part of the input tax that related to non-exempt supplies can be reclaimed.

TAX POINTS

The time of supply, known as the 'tax point', is the date when a transaction takes place for VAT purposes. This date is not necessarily the date the supply physically takes place.

Generally, a VAT-registered business must pay or reclaim VAT in the (usually quarterly) VAT period, or tax period, in which the time of supply occurs, and it must use the correct rate of VAT in force on that date. This means knowing the time of supply/tax point for every transaction is important, as it must be put on the right VAT Return.

Time of supply (tax point) for goods and services

The time of supply for VAT purposes is defined as follows.

- For transactions where no VAT invoice is issued, the time of supply is normally the date the supply takes place (as defined below).

- For transactions where there is a VAT invoice, the time of supply is normally the date the invoice is issued, even if this is after the date the supply took place (as defined below).

To issue a VAT invoice, it must be sent (by post, email etc) or given to the customer for them to keep. A tax point cannot be created simply by preparing an invoice.

However there are exceptions to these rules on time of supply, detailed below.

Date the supply takes place

For goods, the time when the goods are considered to be supplied for VAT purposes is the date when one of the following happens.

- The supplier sends the goods to the customer.

- The customer collects the goods from the supplier.

- The goods (which are not either sent or collected) are made available for the customer to use, for example if the supplier is assembling something on the customer's premises.

For services, the date when the services are supplied for VAT purposes is the date when the service is carried out and all the work – except invoicing – is finished.

Exceptions regarding time of supply (tax point)

The above general principles for working out the time of supply do not apply in the following situations.

- For transactions where a VAT invoice is issued, or payment is received, in advance of the date of supply, the time of supply is the date the invoice is issued or the payment is received, whichever is the earlier.

- If the supplier receives full payment before the date when the supply takes place and no VAT invoice has yet been issued, the time of supply is the date the payment is received.

- If the supplier receives part-payment before the date when the supply takes place, the time of supply becomes the date the part-payment is received but only for the amount of the part-payment (assuming no VAT invoice has been issued before this date – in which case the time of supply is the date the invoice is issued). The time of supply for the remainder will follow the normal rules and might fall in a different VAT period, and so have to go onto a different VAT Return.

- If the supplier issues a VAT invoice more than 14 days after the date when the supply took place, the time of supply will be the date the supply took place, and not the date the invoice is issued. However, if a supplier has genuine commercial difficulties in invoicing within 14 days of the supply taking place, they can contact HMRC to ask for permission to issue invoices later than 14 days and move the time of supply to this later date.

VAT INVOICES

To whom is a VAT invoice issued?

Whenever a VAT-registered business supplies taxable goods or services to another VAT-registered business, it must give the customer a VAT invoice.

A VAT-registered business is not required to issue a VAT invoice to a non VAT-registered business or to a member of the public, but it must do so if requested.

What is a VAT invoice?

A VAT invoice shows certain VAT details of a supply of goods or services. It can be either in paper or electronic form.

A VAT-registered customer must have a valid VAT invoice from the supplier in order to claim back the VAT they have paid on the purchase for their business.

What is NOT a VAT invoice?

The following are NOT VAT invoices:

- Pro forma invoices
- Invoices for only zero-rated or exempt supplies
- Invoices that state 'this is not a VAT invoice'
- Statements of account
- Delivery notes
- Orders
- Letters, emails or other correspondence

A registered business cannot reclaim the VAT it has paid on a purchase by using these documents as proof of payment.

What a VAT invoice must show

A VAT invoice must show:

- An invoice number which is unique and follows on from the number of the previous invoice – any spoiled or cancelled serially numbered invoice must be kept to show to a VAT officer at the next VAT inspection

- The seller's name or trading name, and address

- The seller's VAT registration number

- The invoice date

- The time of supply or tax point if this is different from the invoice date

- The customer's name or trading name, and address

- A description sufficient to identify the goods or services supplied to the customer

For each different type of item listed on the invoice, the business must show:

- The unit price or rate, excluding VAT
- The quantity of goods or the extent of the services
- The rate of VAT that applies to what is being sold
- The total amount payable, excluding VAT
- The rate of any cash or settlement discount
- The total amount of VAT charged

If the business issues a VAT invoice that includes zero-rated or exempt goods or services, it must:

- Show clearly that there is no VAT payable on those goods or services
- Show the total of those values separately

Rounding on VAT invoices

The total VAT payable on all goods and services shown on a VAT invoice may be rounded to a whole penny. Any fraction of a penny can be ignored. (This concession is not available to retailers.)

Time limits for issuing VAT invoices

There is a strict time limit on issuing VAT invoices. Normally a VAT invoice to a VAT-registered customer must be issued within 30 days of the date of supply of the goods or services or, if the business was paid in advance, the date payment was received. This is so the customer can claim back the VAT on the supply, if they are entitled to do so.

Invoices cannot be issued any later without permission from HMRC, except in a few limited circumstances.

A valid VAT invoice is needed to reclaim VAT

Even if a business is registered for VAT, it can normally only reclaim VAT on purchases if:

- They are for use in the business or for business purposes and
- A valid VAT invoice for the purchase is received and retained.

Only VAT-registered businesses can issue valid VAT invoices. A business cannot reclaim VAT on any goods or services that are purchased from a business that is not VAT-registered.

Where simplified (less detailed) VAT invoices can be issued

Simplified VAT invoices

If a VAT-registered business makes taxable supplies of goods or services for £250 or less including VAT, then it can issue a simplified (less detailed) VAT invoice that only needs to show:

- The seller's name and address
- The seller's VAT registration number
- The time of supply (tax point)
- A description of the goods or services
- The total payable including VAT

If the supply includes items at different VAT rates then, for each different VAT rate, the simplified VAT invoice must also show the VAT rate applicable to the item(s).

Exempt supplies must not be included on a simplified VAT invoice.

If the business accepts credit cards, then it can create a simplified invoice by adapting the sales voucher given to the cardholder when the sale is made. It must show the information described above.

There is no requirement for the business making the supply to keep copies of any less detailed invoices it has issued.

Pro forma invoices

If there is a need to issue a sales document for goods or services not supplied yet, the business can issue a 'pro forma' invoice or a similar document as part of the offer to supply goods or services to customers.

A pro forma invoice is not a VAT invoice, and it should be clearly marked with the words 'This is not a VAT invoice'.

If a potential customer accepts the goods or services offered to them and these are actually supplied, then a VAT invoice must be issued within the appropriate time limit if appropriate.

If the business has been issued with a pro forma invoice by a supplier it cannot be used to claim back VAT on the purchase. A VAT invoice must be obtained from the supplier.

Advance payments or deposits

An advance payment, or deposit, is a proportion of the total selling price that a customer pays before they are supplied with goods or services. When a business asks for an advance payment, the tax point is whichever of the following happens first:

- The date a VAT invoice is issued for the advance payment
- The date the advance payment is received

The business must include the VAT on the advance payment on the VAT Return for the period when the tax point occurs.

If the customer pays the remaining balance before the goods are delivered or the services are performed, another tax point is created when whichever of the following happens first:

- A VAT invoice is issued for the balance
- Payment of the balance is received

The VAT on the balance must be included on the VAT Return for the period when the tax point occurs.

Discounts on goods and services

If any goods or services supplied by a VAT-registered business are discounted, VAT is charged on the discounted price rather than the full price.

When a business makes an offer to a customer such as 'we will pay your VAT', VAT is actually payable to HMRC on the amount the customer would have paid on the discounted price, not the amount they have paid at the full price.

Returned goods, credit notes, debit notes and VAT

For a buyer who has received a VAT invoice

If goods are returned to the seller for a full or partial credit there are three options:

- Return the invoice to the supplier and obtain a replacement invoice showing the proper amount of VAT due, if any
- Obtain a credit note from the supplier
- Issue a debit note to the supplier

If the buyer issues a debit note or receives a credit note, it must:

- Record this in the accounting records
- Enter it on the next VAT Return, deducting the VAT on the credit or debit note from the amount of VAT which can be reclaimed

For a seller who has issued a VAT invoice

If goods are returned by a customer, there are again three options:

- Cancel and recover the original invoice, and issue a replacement showing the correct amount of any VAT due, if any
- Issue a credit note to the customer
- Obtain a debit note from the customer

If the seller issues a credit note or receives a debit note, it must:

- Record this in the accounting records
- Enter it on the next VAT Return, deducting the VAT on the credit or debit note from the amount of VAT payable

ENTERTAINMENT EXPENSES

Business entertainment

Business entertainment is any form of free or subsidised entertainment or hospitality to non-employees, for example suppliers and customers. Generally a business cannot reclaim input tax on business entertainment expenses. The exception is that input tax can be reclaimed in respect of entertaining overseas customers, but not UK or Isle of Man customers.

Employee expenses and entertainment

The business can, however, reclaim VAT on employee expenses and employee entertainment expenses if those expenses relate to travel and subsistence or where the entertainment applies only to employees.

Generally, when the entertainment is in respect of both employees and non-employees, the business can only reclaim VAT on the proportion of the expenses that is for employees. The business is also permitted to recover input tax on the cost of entertainment incurred in respect of non-employees who are customers from outside the EU.

VEHICLES AND MOTORING EXPENSES

VAT and vehicles

When it buys a car a registered business generally cannot reclaim the VAT. There are some exceptions – for example, when the car is used mainly as one of the following:

- A taxi
- For driving instruction
- For self-drive hire

If the VAT on the original purchase price of a car bought new is not reclaimed, the business does not have to charge any VAT when it is sold. This is because the sale of the car is exempt for VAT purposes. If the business did reclaim the VAT when it bought the car new, VAT is chargeable when it comes to sell it.

VAT-registered businesses can generally reclaim the VAT when they buy a commercial vehicle such as a van, lorry or tractor.

Reclaiming VAT on road fuel

If the business pays for road fuel, it can deal with the VAT charged on the fuel in one of four ways:

- Reclaim all of the VAT. All of the fuel must be used only for business purposes.

- Reclaim all of the VAT and pay the appropriate fuel scale charge – this is a way of accounting for output tax on fuel that the business buys but that is then used for private motoring.

- Reclaim only the VAT that relates to fuel used for business mileage. Detailed records of business and private mileage must be kept.

- Do not reclaim any VAT. This can be a useful option if mileage is low and also if fuel is used for both business and private motoring. If the business chooses this option it must apply it to all vehicles, including commercial vehicles.

TRANSACTIONS OUTSIDE THE UK

Exports, despatches and supplying goods abroad: charging VAT

If a business sells, supplies or transfers goods out of the UK to someone in another country it may need to charge VAT on them.

Generally speaking, the business can zero-rate supplies exported outside the European Union (EU), or sent to someone who is registered for VAT in another EU member state, provided it follows strict rules, obtains and keeps the necessary evidence, and obeys all laws.

Goods supplied to another EU member state are technically known as despatches rather than exports. The term 'exports' is reserved to describe sales to a country outside the EU.

VAT on despatches of goods to someone who is not VAT registered in another EU member state

When a business supplies goods to someone in another EU member state, and they are not registered for VAT in that member state, it should normally charge VAT.

VAT on despatches of goods to someone who is VAT registered in another EU member state

If, however, goods are supplied to someone who is registered for VAT in the destination EU member state, the business can zero-rate the supply for VAT purposes, provided it meets certain conditions.

VAT on exports of goods to non-EU countries

VAT is a tax charged on goods used in the European Union (EU), so if goods are exported outside the EU, VAT is not charged, and the supply can be zero-rated.

Imports, acquisitions and purchasing goods from abroad: paying and reclaiming VAT

Generally speaking, VAT is payable on all purchases of goods that are bought from abroad at the same rate that would apply to the goods if bought in the UK. The business must tell HMRC about goods that it imports, and pay any VAT and duty that is due.

VAT on goods acquired from EU member states

If a business is registered for VAT in the UK and buys goods from inside the EU, these are known as acquisitions rather than imports. Usually no VAT is charged by the supplier but acquisition tax, at the same rate of VAT that would apply if the goods were supplied in the UK, is due on the acquisition. This is reclaimed as input tax as if the goods were bought in the UK.

VAT on imports of goods from non-EU countries

VAT may be charged on imports of goods bought from non-EU countries. The business can reclaim any VAT paid on the goods imported as input tax.

BAD DEBTS

When a business can reclaim VAT on bad debts

VAT that has been paid to HMRC and which has not been received from the customer can be reclaimed as bad debt relief. The conditions are that:

- The debt is more than six months and less than four years and six months overdue

- The debt has been written off in the VAT account and transferred to a separate bad debt account

- The debt has not been sold or handed to a factoring company

- The business did not charge more than the normal selling price for the items

Bad debt relief does not apply when the cash accounting scheme is used because the VAT is not paid to HMRC until after the customer has paid it to the supplier.

How to claim bad debt relief

If the business is entitled to claim bad debt relief, add the amount of VAT to be reclaimed to the amount of VAT being reclaimed on purchases (input tax) and put the total figure in Box 4 of the VAT Return.

COMPLETING THE VAT RETURN, BOX BY BOX

Extracted as relevant from VAT Notice 700/12 updated 20/08/2014

The online VAT Return where no VAT Accounting Scheme is used is completed as follows:

Box 1 – VAT due in this period on sales and other outputs

Include the VAT due on all goods and services you supplied in the period covered by the return. This is your 'output VAT' (or 'output tax') for the period. VAT may also be due on supplies outside the mainstream of your business. Some examples are:

- Fuel used for private motoring where VAT is accounted for using a scale charge.

Points to remember when filling in box 1:

- Deduct any VAT on credit notes issued by you.

- You can sometimes include VAT underdeclared/overdeclared on previous returns.

- You must not declare zero-rated exports or supplies to other EC member states.

Box 2 – VAT due in this period on acquisitions from other member states of the European Community (EC)

Show the VAT due on all goods and related costs purchased from VAT registered suppliers in other EC member states. You may also be entitled to reclaim this mount as input VAT and do so by including the relevant figure within the total at box 4.

Box 3 – Total VAT due

Show the total VAT due, that is, boxes 1 and 2 added together.

Box 4 – VAT reclaimed in this period on purchases and other inputs (including acquisitions from the EC)

Show the total amount of deductible VAT charged on your business purchases. This is referred to as your 'input VAT' (or 'input tax') for the period.

You can reclaim VAT:

- You can reclaim on acquisitions of goods from VAT registered suppliers in other EC member states (this must correspond with the amount declared within box 2).

- You are claiming back as bad debt relief.

Points to remember when filling in box 4:

Make sure you do not include VAT:

- You pay on goods bought wholly for your personal use.
- On business entertainment expenses.

Other points to remember:

- Deduct VAT on any credit notes issued to you.

- You can sometimes include VAT underdeclared/overdeclared on previous returns.

- If you are partly exempt your recovery of input VAT is subject to partial exemption rules.

Box 5 – Net VAT to be paid to HMRC or reclaimed

Take the figures in boxes 3 and 4. Deduct the smaller from the larger and enter the difference in box 5.

Box 6 – Total value of sales and all other outputs excluding any VAT

Show the total value of all your business sales and other specific outputs but leave out any VAT.

Some examples are:

- Zero-rate, reduced-rate and exempt supplies
- Exports
- Supplies to other EC member states (that is any figure entered in box 8)
- Deposits for which an invoice has been issued

Box 7 – Total value of purchases and all other inputs excluding any VAT

Show the total value of your purchases and expenses but leave out any VAT.

You must include the value of:

- Imports
- Acquisition from VAT registered suppliers in other EC member states (that is any figure entered in box 9)

Box 8 – Total value of all supplies of goods and related costs, excluding any VAT, to other EC member states

Show the total value of all supplies of goods to other EC member states and directly related costs, such as freight and insurance, where these form part of the invoice or contract price. Leave out any VAT.

Box 9 – Total value of acquisitions of goods and related costs, excluding any VAT, from other EC member states

Show the total value of all acquisitions of goods from VAT registered suppliers in other EC Member States and directly related costs, such as freight and insurance, where these form part of the invoice or contract price, but leave out any VAT.

VAT PERIODS, SUBMITTING RETURNS AND PAYING VAT

VAT Returns for transactions to the end of the relevant VAT period must be submitted by the due date shown on the VAT Return. VAT due must also be paid by the due date.

What is a VAT period?

A VAT period is the period of time over which the business records VAT transactions in the VAT account for completion of the VAT Return. The VAT period is three months (a quarter) unless the annual accounting scheme is used. The end dates of a business's four VAT periods are determined when it first registers for VAT, but it can choose to amend the dates on which its VAT periods end. This is often done to match VAT periods to accounting period ends.

Submitting VAT Returns online and paying HMRC electronically

It is mandatory for virtually all VAT-registered traders to submit their VAT Returns to HMRC using online filing, and to pay HMRC electronically.

Due dates for submitting the VAT Return and paying electronically

Businesses are responsible for calculating how much VAT they owe and for paying VAT so that the amount clears to HMRC's bank account on or before the due date. Paying on time avoids having to pay a surcharge for late payment.

The normal due date for submitting each VAT Return and electronically paying HMRC any VAT that is owed is one calendar month after the end of the relevant VAT period, unless the annual accounting scheme is operated. The normal due date for the return and payment can be found on the return.

Online filing and electronic payment mean that businesses get an extended due date for filing the return of seven extra calendar days after the normal due date shown on the VAT Return. This extra seven days also applies to paying HMRC so that the amount has cleared to HMRC's bank account. However this does not apply in these exceptional cases:

- The business uses the Annual Accounting Scheme for VAT

- The business is required to make payments on account (unless it submits monthly returns)

If the business pays HMRC by Direct Debit, HMRC automatically collects payment from the business's bank account three bank working days after the extra seven calendar days following the normal due date.

If the business does not manage to pay cleared funds into HMRC's bank account by the payment deadline, or fails to have sufficient funds in its account to meet the direct debit, it may be liable to a surcharge for late payment.

Repayment of VAT

If the amount of VAT reclaimed (entered in Box 4) is more than the VAT to be paid (entered in Box 3), then the net VAT value in Box 5 is a repayment due to the business from HMRC.

HMRC is obliged to schedule this sum for repayment automatically, provided checks applied to the VAT Return do not indicate that such a repayment might not be due. There may be circumstances when the business does not receive the repayment automatically, for instance if there is an outstanding debt owed to HMRC.

SPECIAL ACCOUNTING SCHEMES

Annual Accounting Scheme for VAT

Using standard VAT accounting, four VAT Returns each year are required. Any VAT due is payable quarterly, and any VAT refunds due are also receivable quarterly.

Using the normal annual accounting scheme, the business makes nine interim payments at monthly intervals. There is only one VAT Return to complete, at the end of the year, when either a balancing payment is made or a balancing refund is received.

Businesses can start on the annual accounting scheme if their estimated taxable turnover during the next tax year is not more than £1.35 million. Businesses already using the annual accounting scheme can continue to do so until the estimated taxable turnover for the next tax year exceeds £1.6 million.

Whilst using the annual accounting scheme the business may also be able to use either the cash accounting scheme or the flat rate scheme, but not both.

Benefits of annual accounting

- One VAT Return per year, instead of four.

- Two months after the tax period end to complete and send in the annual VAT Return and pay the balance of VAT payable, rather than the usual one month.

- Better management of cash flow by paying a fixed amount in nine instalments.

- Ability to make additional payments as and when required.

- Join from VAT registration day, or at any other time if already registered for VAT.

Disadvantages of annual accounting

- Only one repayment per year, which is not beneficial if the business regularly requires refunds.

- If turnover decreases, interim payments may be higher than the VAT payments would be under standard VAT accounting – again there is a need to wait until the end of the year to receive a refund.

Cash Accounting Scheme for VAT

Using standard VAT accounting, VAT is paid on sales within a VAT period whether or not the customer has paid. Using cash accounting, VAT is not paid until the customer has paid the invoice. If a customer never pays, the business never has to pay the VAT.

Cash accounting can be used if the estimated taxable turnover during the next tax year is not more than £1.35 million. A business can continue to use cash accounting until its taxable turnover exceeds £1.6 million.

The cash accounting scheme may be used in conjunction with the annual accounting scheme but not with the flat rate scheme.

Benefits of cash accounting

Using cash accounting may help cash flow, especially if customers are slow payers. Payment of VAT is not made until the business has received payment from the customer, so if a customer never pays, VAT does not have to be paid on that bad debt as long as the business is using the cash accounting scheme.

Disadvantages of cash accounting

Using cash accounting may adversely affect cash flow:

- The business cannot reclaim VAT on purchases until it has paid for them. This can be a disadvantage if most goods and services are purchased on credit.

- Businesses which regularly reclaim more VAT than they pay will usually receive repayment later under cash accounting than under standard VAT accounting, unless they pay for everything at the time of purchase.

- If a business starts using cash accounting when it starts trading, it will not be able to reclaim VAT on most start-up expenditure, such as initial stock, tools or machinery, until it has actually paid for those items.

- When it leaves the cash accounting scheme the business will have to account for all outstanding VAT due, including on any bad debts.

Flat Rate Scheme for VAT

If its VAT-exclusive taxable turnover is less than £150,000 per year, the business could simplify its VAT accounting by registering on the Flat Rate Scheme and calculating VAT payments as a percentage of its total VAT-inclusive turnover. There is no reclaim of VAT on purchases – this is taken into account in calculating the flat rate percentage that applies to the business. The flat rate scheme can reduce the time needed in accounting for and working out VAT. Even though the business still needs to show a VAT amount on each VAT invoice, it does not need to record how much VAT it charged on every sale in its accounts. Nor does it need to record the VAT paid on every purchase.

Once on the scheme, the business can continue to use it until its total business income exceeds £230,000. The flat rate scheme may be used in conjunction with the annual accounting scheme but not the cash accounting scheme.

Benefits of using the flat rate scheme

Using the flat rate scheme can save time and smooth cash flow. It offers these benefits:

- No need to record the VAT charged on every sale and purchase, as with standard VAT accounting. This can save time. But although the business only has to pay HMRC a percentage of its turnover, it must still show VAT at the appropriate normal rate (standard, reduced or zero) on the VAT invoices it issues.

- A first year discount. A business in its first year of VAT registration gets a 1% reduction in the applicable flat rate percentage until the day before the first anniversary of VAT registration.

- Fewer rules to follow, for instance no longer having to work out what VAT on purchases can or cannot be reclaimed.

- Peace of mind. With less chance of mistakes, there are fewer worries about getting the VAT right.

- Certainty. The business always knows what percentage of takings has to be paid to HMRC.

Potential disadvantages of using the flat rate scheme

The flat rate percentages are calculated in a way that takes into account zero-rated and exempt sales. They also contain an allowance for the VAT spent on purchases. So the VAT Flat Rate Scheme might not be right for the business if:

- It buys mostly standard-rated items, as there is no reclaim of any VAT on purchases

- It regularly receives a VAT repayment under standard VAT accounting

- It makes a lot of zero-rated or exempt sales

ERRORS IN PREVIOUS VAT RETURNS

Action to be taken at the end of the VAT period

At the end of the VAT period, the business should calculate the net value of all the errors and omissions found during the period that relate to VAT Returns already submitted – that is, any tax which should have been claimed back is subtracted from any additional tax due to HMRC. Any deliberate errors must not be included – these must be separately declared to HMRC.

What the business should do next depends on whether the net value of all the errors is less than or greater than the 'error correction reporting threshold', which is the greater of:

- £10,000

- 1% of the box 6 figure on the VAT Return for the period when the error was discovered – subject to an upper limit of £50,000

If the net value of all the errors is less than the error reporting threshold then, if preferred, the errors may be corrected by making an adjustment on the current VAT Return (Method 1).

However, if the value of the net VAT error discovered is above this threshold, it must be declared to HMRC separately, in writing (Method 2). This also applies if the error is for an accounting period that ended more than four years ago.

How to adjust the VAT Return: Method 1

Errors from previous VAT Returns can be corrected by adjusting the VAT liability on the current VAT Return if the net value is below the error correction reporting threshold.

At the end of the VAT period when the errors are discovered, the VAT account of output tax due or input tax claimed is adjusted by the net amount of all errors. The VAT account must show the amount of the adjustment being made to the VAT Return.

To work out the net value of the errors:

- Add up the additional tax due to HMRC
- Subtract the tax due from HMRC

When the next return is submitted, add the net value of the error to Box 1 for tax due to HMRC, or to Box 4 for tax due from HMRC.

For example, if the business discovers that it did not account for VAT payable to HMRC of £100 on a supply made in the past, and also did not account for £60 VAT reclaimable on a purchase, it should add £40 to the Box 1 figure on the current VAT Return.

How to separately declare an error to HMRC: Method 2

For certain errors a separate declaration is required to the relevant HMRC VAT Error Correction Team in writing about the mistake. The simplest way to tell them is to use Form VAT 652 "Notification of Errors in VAT Returns", which is for reporting errors on previous returns, but the business does not have to use Form VAT 652 – it can simply write a letter instead.

Businesses may, if they wish, use this method for errors of any size, even those which are below the error reporting threshold ie instead of a Method 1 error correction. Using this method means the business must not make adjustment for the same errors on a later VAT Return.

Method 2 must always be used if the net error exceeds the error reporting threshold or if the errors made on previous returns were made deliberately.

SURCHARGES, PENALTIES AND ASSESSMENTS

Surcharges for missed VAT Return or VAT payment deadlines

VAT-registered businesses must submit a VAT Return and pay any VAT by the relevant due date. If HMRC receives a return or VAT payment after the due date, the business is 'in default' and may have to pay a surcharge in addition to the VAT that is owed.

The first default is dealt with by a warning known as a 'Surcharge Liability Notice'. This notice tells the business that if it submits or pays late ('defaults') again during the following 12 months – known as the surcharge period – it may be charged a surcharge.

Submitting or paying late again during the surcharge period could result in a 'default surcharge'. This is a percentage of any unpaid VAT owed. Where a correct return is not submitted at all, HMRC will estimate the amount of VAT owed and base the surcharge on that amount (this is known as an assessment – see below).

HMRC assessments

Businesses have a legal obligation to submit VAT Returns and pay any VAT owed to HMRC by the relevant due date. If they do not submit a return, HMRC can issue an assessment which shows the amount of VAT that HMRC believes it is owed, based on HMRC's best estimate.

Penalties for careless and deliberate errors

Careless and deliberate errors will be liable to a penalty, whether they are adjusted on the VAT Return or separately declared.

If a business discovers an error which is neither careless nor deliberate, HMRC expects that it will take steps to adjust or declare it, as appropriate. If the business fails to take such steps, the inaccuracy will be treated as careless and a penalty will be due.

Penalties for inaccurate returns

Penalties may be applied if a VAT Return is inaccurate, and correcting this means tax is unpaid, understated, over-claimed or under-assessed. Telling HMRC about inaccuracies as soon as the business is aware of them may reduce any penalty that is due, in some cases to zero.

Penalty for late registration

Failure to register for VAT with HMRC at the right time may make a business liable to a late registration penalty.

FINDING OUT MORE INFORMATION ABOUT VAT

Most questions can be answered by referring to the VAT section of the HMRC website.

VAT Enquiries Helpline

If the answer to a question is not on the HMRC website, the quickest and easiest way is to ring the VAT Enquiries Helpline where most VAT questions can be answered.

Letters to HMRC

The VAT Enquiries Helpline can answer most questions relating to VAT, but there may be times when it is more appropriate to write to HMRC.

This would apply if:

- The VAT information published by HMRC – either on the website or in printed notices and information sheets – has not answered a question

- The VAT Enquiries Helpline has asked the business to write

- There is real doubt about how VAT affects a particular transaction, personal situation or business

If HMRC already publishes information that answers the question, their response will give the relevant details.

VISITS BY VAT OFFICERS

VAT officers are responsible for the collection of VAT for the government. They check businesses to make sure that their VAT records are up to date. They also check that amounts claimed from or paid to the government are correct. They examine VAT records, question the business owner or the person responsible for the VAT records, and watch business activity.

Notes

Notes

Notes

Notes

Notes

Notes

REVIEW FORM

How have you used this Text?
(Tick one box only)

☐ Home study

☐ On a course_____

☐ Other _____

Why did you decide to purchase this Text? *(Tick one box only)*

☐ Have used BPP Texts in the past

☐ Recommendation by friend/colleague

☐ Recommendation by a college lecturer

☐ Saw advertising

☐ Other _____

During the past six months do you recall seeing/receiving either of the following?
(Tick as many boxes as are relevant)

☐ Our advertisement in Accounting Technician

☐ Our Publishing Catalogue

Which (if any) aspects of our advertising do you think are useful?
(Tick as many boxes as are relevant)

☐ Prices and publication dates of new editions

☐ Information on Text content

☐ Details of our free online offering

☐ None of the above

Your ratings, comments and suggestions would be appreciated on the following areas of this Text.

	Very useful	Useful	Not useful
Introductory section	☐	☐	☐
Quality of explanations	☐	☐	☐
How it works	☐	☐	☐
Chapter tasks	☐	☐	☐
Chapter overviews	☐	☐	☐
Test your learning	☐	☐	☐
Index	☐	☐	☐

	Excellent	Good	Adequate	Poor
Overall opinion of this Text	☐	☐	☐	☐

Do you intend to continue using BPP Products? ☐ Yes ☐ No

Please note any further comments and suggestions/errors on the reverse of this page. The range manager of this edition can be emailed at: nisarahmed@bpp.com

Please return to: Nisar Ahmed, Head of Programme, BPP Learning Media Ltd, FREEPOST, London, W12 8AA.

REVIEW FORM (continued)

TELL US WHAT YOU THINK

Please note any further comments and suggestions/errors below